CONTENTS

INTRODUCTION

The instant pot air fryer lid is one of the advanced and revolutionary cooking appliances available on the market. Using this revolutionary cooking gadget, you can easily convert your instant pot into an advanced air fryer by just swapping the instant pot and air fryer lid. The instant pot air fryer lid does not just save the countertop space of your kitchen but also saves you time and money. It performs 6 different cooking appliance functions in a single appliance. You never need to buy another appliance just fix the air fryer lid to a 6-quart instant pot model. Most of the 6-quart models are comfortable for an air fryer lid. The instant pot air fryer lid works on hot air circulation technology. It blows very hot air (400°F) into an instant pot cooking chamber to cook your food quickly and evenly from all sides.

The instant pot air fryer lid comes with various different air frying functions like air fry, roast, broil, bake, dehydrate and also reheats your food. If you are one of those people who like fried food but are worried about extra calories then this is the right appliance for you. It cooks your food using very little oil. If you want to fry a bowl of French fries just sprinkle a tablespoon of oil over it and your air fryer lid makes your French fries crisp from outside and tender from inside. Cooking your food with an instant pot air fryer lid is one of the healthiest, easiest and safest way of cooking. After finishing cooking it is easy to clean.

The instant pot air fryer lid allows you to cook lots of dishes like Breakfasts, Snacks and Appetizers, Soup and Stew, Vegetarian, Poultry, Pork, Beef and Lamb, Fish and Seafood to Desserts. The book contains 250 varied authentic, healthy, delicious and tasty recipes. All the recipes that are written in this book are easy to understand and made up from simple ingredients which are available in your kitchen. All the recipes come with their exact preparation time and cooking time with their exact nutritional values.

My goal here is to introduce you to the versatile and advanced cooking appliance popularly known as the instant pot air fryer lid. All the healthy and delicious recipes written in this book are prepared and well tested. I hope you enjoy all the healthy, delicious and tasty recipes from this book using the instant pot air fryer lid. There are various different types of books available on the market on this topic; thanks for choosing my book. The information found in this book may definitely help you in your daily cooking process.

Cooking with Instant Pot Air Fryer Lid

The instant pot air fryer lid is one of the advanced portable cooking tools that make your daily cooking easy. It converts your instant pot into an air fryer by a simple switch of lids. The instant pot air fryer lid is easily fixed with most of the selected six-quart instant pot models. The lid allows you to transform your instant pot into an advanced air fryer which performs different air fryer operations. It fries crispy French fries, bakes a cake and a cookie, broils burgers, roasts your favorite meat or chicken, dehydrates your favorite fruit slices and also reheats your frozen foods. It converts your instant pot into a multi-cooking kitchen appliance by just swapping the instant pot lid with an air fryer lid.

When you are using an instant pot air fryer lid it is recommended that the lid is used only with a stainless-steel inner pot, do not use a ceramic pot with this air fryer lid. The air fryer lid works as a duo crisp air fryer lid, it comes with the heating element and blower fan, it circulates very hot air into your air fryer to air fry your food quickly and evenly from all sides. The instant pot air fryer lid comes with 6 pre-programmed functions preset on the top side of the lid with a digital display. While using these presets you never need to worry about time and temperature settings because these functions are preset perfect temperature and exact time. You just need to select the desired button and press the start button to run the program as per your requirement. Without pressing the start button your program never runs. These 6 preset functions are:

Air Fry: This function is used to make your food crisp. Using this function, you can make your French fries crisp from outside and tender on the inside. It can also be used to crisp your frozen food and pressure-cooked dishes.

Roast: This function is used to roast your chicken and also gives a nice crisp and crust to your favorite food.

Bake: This function helps to bake your favorite cake, brownie, and delicious cookies.

Broil: This function is used to melt cheese over pasta, broils your favorite burger, browns foods like chicken, and also cooks your favorite meat cuts.

Dehydrate: This function runs on low heat for a long time period. Using this function, you can dehydrate your favorite fruit slice. This function only dries it out not to cook, it just spreads warm air into the air fryer to remove the moisture from the air fryer. You can make crispy apple chips at home using this function.

Reheat: This function is used to reheat your frozen food, or it can make your food crisp as the night before.

You can easily pressure cook your favorite food in the instant pot and give it a nice brown and crisp texture using this cook and crisp technology. This magical cooking appliance not only saves your kitchen top space but also saves you money and time. You never need to purchase another appliance for a single operation like broil, bake, reheat, air fry, roast, and dehydrate. An instant pot air fryer lid is one of the appliances that come with two lids; one is for pressure cooking purposes and the other is for air frying your food. This two-lid appliance gives you an amazing cooking experience just swapping the lids.

How to use the instant pot air fryer lid

The instant pot air fryer lid is easy to operate; all the functions are given on the top side of the lid along with the digital display. If you are a new user then follow the step by step instructions given below to operate the instant pot lid in the proper way.

Step 1: Make sure your instant pot is unplugged. If there is pressure in the pot then release it and remove the regular pressure cooking lid from the instant pot.

Step 2: Then place your instant pot air fryer lid over the top of the stainless-steel inner pot (recommended use only stainless-steel inner pot, do not use ceramic inner pot while using air fryer lid) and lock the lid.

Step 3: Plug your air fryer lid into the socket and select the program from the top of the air fryer lid as per your recipe requirements. You can also increase or decrease the time and temperature setting as per your recipe needs by just pressing the + and – setting button.

Step 4: Press the Start button to start the cooking process. When the cooking process has completed its half cooking cycle the display indicates a "Turn Food" message to turn your food.

Step 5: If you want to turn the food open the lid and turn your food. When you open the lid the program automatically stops and resumes when the lid is locked. If you don't want to turn your food just ignore the message it will automatically resume the cooking process after a 10 second wait.

Step 6: When the cooking process has completed then the display shows the message "End Cool". At this stage, your cooking process has completed and you should remove the air fryer lid and place it over the gray protective pad.

Using these simple steps, you can cook a variety of different healthy, delicious and tasty dishes in your kitchen with less effort.

Instant pot models suitable with air fryer lid

The instant pot air fryer lid is only suitable with 6-quart instant pot models these comfortable models are

DUO60 models (DUO Teal 60, DUO Red 60, DUO Dazzling Dahlia 60, DUO White 60, DUO Nova Black SS 60, IP-DUO60-ENW, IP-DUO60, IP-DUO60 V2, IP-DUO60 V2.1, IP-DUO60 V3, DUO 60 V3, DUO Red SS 60, DUO Black SS 60, DUO Frontier Rose 60**)**

LUX60 models (IP-LUX60 V2, IP-LUX60-ENW-MM, IP-LUX60 V3, LUX60 V3, LUX Breezy Blossoms 60, LUX Vintage Floral 60, LUX Red SS 60, LUX Black SS 60, IP-LUX60, LUX Red 60, LUX Blue 60**)**

NOVA PLUS 60 models (DUO Plus Black SS 60, DUO Plus Copper SS 60, DUO Plus 60, DUO Plus Blue SS 60, DUO Plus Cinnamon SS 60**)**

VIVA 60 models (Viva Black SS 60 Viva Red SS 60, Viva Black SS 60 Viva Red SS 60**), DUO PLUS 60 and DUO NOVA 60**

BREAKFAST RECIPES

1-Breakfast Potatoes

Cook time: 25 minutes | Serves: 3 | Per Serving: Calories 167, Carbs 24.3g, Fat 7.2g, Protein 2.7g

Ingredients:

- Russet potatoes – 1 pound, peeled & cut into ½-inch pieces
- Fresh parsley – 1/2 tbsp., chopped
- Onion powder – ¼ tsp.
- Paprika – ¼ tsp.
- Garlic powder – ¼ tsp.
- Olive oil – 1 ½ tbsps.
- Pepper & salt, to taste

Directions:

Add potatoes into the large bowl. Add remaining ingredients over potatoes except for the parsley and toss well. Add potatoes into the multi-level air fryer basket and place basket into the instant pot. Seal pot with air fryer lid. Select bake mode and cook at 380 F for 25 minutes. Stir potatoes halfway through. Garnish with parsley and serve.

2-Cheesy Breakfast Eggs

Cook time: 15 minutes | Serves: 1 | Per Serving: Calories 358, Carbs 2g, Fat 28g, Protein 22g

Ingredients:

- Eggs – 2
- Parmesan cheese – 1 tbsp., grated
- Cheddar cheese – 2 tbsps., shredded
- Heavy cream – 2 tbsps.
- Pepper & salt, to taste

Directions:

Spray one ramekin with cooking spray and set aside. In a small bowl, whisk eggs with heavy cream. Add remaining ingredients and stir well. Pour egg mixture into the prepared ramekin. Place the dehydrating tray into the multi-level air fryer basket and place basket into the instant pot. Place the ramekin on dehydrating tray. Seal pot with the air fryer lid. Select bake mode and cook at 380 F for 15-20 minutes or until eggs are set. Serve.

3-Breakfast Egg Bite

Cook time: 15 minutes | Serves: 8 | Per Serving: Calories 120, Carbs 2g, Fat 9g, Protein 8g

Ingredients:

- Eggs – 6
- Bacon slices – 3, cooked and crumbled
- Mozzarella cheese – 4 tbsps., shredded
- Cheddar cheese – ½ cup, shredded

- Spinach – ¼ cup, chopped
- Onion – ¼ cup, chopped
- Bell peppers – ½ cup, chopped
- Onions – ¼ cup, chopped
- Heavy cream– 2 tbsps.
- Pepper & salt, to taste

Directions:

In a mixing bowl, whisk eggs with heavy cream, pepper, and salt. Add remaining ingredients and stir everything well. Pour egg mixture into the 8 silicone muffin molds. Place the dehydrating tray into the multi-level air fryer basket and place basket into the instant pot. Place the 6 silicone molds on the dehydrating tray. Seal pot with the air fryer lid. Select the air fry mode and cook at 300 F for 15 minutes. Cook the 2 remaining egg bites. Serve.

4-Banana Breakfast Muffins

Cook time: 15 minutes │Serves: 10 │ Per Serving: Calories 161, Carbs 22g, Fat 8g, Protein 2g

Ingredients:

- Ripe bananas – 2, mashed
- Self-raising flour – ¾ cup
- Cinnamon – 1 tsp.
- Vanilla – 1 tsp.
- Brown sugar – ½ cup
- Egg – 1
- Olive oil – 1/3 cup

Directions:

In a mixing bowl, beat egg, vanilla, oil, brown sugar, and mashed bananas until combined well. Add flour and cinnamon and mix until combined well. Pour mixture into the 10 silicone muffin molds. Place the dehydrating tray into the multi-level air fryer basket and place basket into the instant pot. Place 6 muffin molds on the dehydrating tray. Seal pot with the air fryer lid. Select air fry mode and cook at 320 F for 15 minutes. Cook remaining muffins. Serve.

5-Delicious Roasted Potatoes

Cook time: 25 minutes │Serves: 2 │ Per Serving: Calories 119, Carbs 21.2g, Fat 2.5g, Protein 4.4g

Ingredients:

- Baby potatoes – 12 oz, cut into chunks
- Olive oil – 1 tsp.
- Italian seasoning – 1 tsp.
- Pepper & salt, to taste

Directions:

Add potatoes into the mixing bowl. Add remaining ingredients and toss well. Add potatoes into the multi-level air fryer basket and place basket into the instant pot.

Seal pot with air fryer lid. Select air fry mode and cook at 400 F for 25 minutes. Stir potatoes twice while cooking. Serve.

6-Almond Flour Donuts

Cook time: 25 minutes │Serves: 6 │ Per Serving: Calories 257, Carbs 5g, Fat 25g, Protein 6g

Ingredients:

- Almond flour – 1 cup
- Vanilla – ½ tsp.
- Eggs – 2
- Almond milk – ¼ cup
- Butter – ¼ cup, melted
- Cinnamon – 1 tsp.
- Baking powder – 2 tsps.
- Erythritol – ¼ cup
- Sea salt– 1/8 tsp.

Directions:

In a mixing bowl, mix together almond flour, cinnamon, baking powder, sweetener, and salt. In a small bowl, whisk together eggs, vanilla, milk, and butter. Pour egg mixture into the almond flour mixture and mix until well combined. Pour batter into the 6 silicone donut molds. Place the dehydrating tray into the multi-level air fryer basket and place basket into the instant pot. Place 4 donut molds on dehydrating tray. Seal pot with air fryer lid. Select bake mode and cook at 350 F for 25 minutes. Cook remaining donuts. Serve.

7-Vegetable Egg Muffins

Cook time: 25 minutes │Serves: 12 │ Per Serving: Calories 144, Carbs 7g, Fat 8g, Protein 10g

Ingredients:

- Mixed vegetables – 3 cups
- Parmesan cheese – 4 tbsps., grated
- Cheddar cheese – 1 cup, shredded
- Onion – 3 tbsps., minced
- Mustard powder – ½ tsp.
- Milk – ¼ cup
- Eggs – 12
- Olive oil – 1 tsp.
- Pepper & salt, to taste

Directions:

Cook mixed vegetables in a pan with 1 tsp olive oil until tender. Remove from heat and set aside. In a mixing bowl, whisk eggs with seasonings, and milk. Add remaining ingredients and mix until well combined. Pour egg mixture into the 12 silicone muffin molds. Place the dehydrating tray into the multi-level air fryer basket and place basket into the instant pot. Place 6 muffin molds on dehydrating tray. Seal pot with air fryer lid. Select bake mode and cook at 350 F for 25 minutes. Cook remaining muffins. Serve.

8-Chia Oat Muffins

Cook time: 15 minutes ⎜Serves: 12 ⎜ Per Serving: Calories 187, Carbs 19.1g, Fat 11.5g, Protein 2.9g

Ingredients:

- Oat flour – 1 ¾ cups
- Chia seeds – 1 tbsp.
- Eggs – 2
- Vanilla – 1 tsp.
- Almond milk – 2 tbsps.
- Fresh lemon juice – 2 tbsps.
- Coconut oil – ½ cup, melted
- Applesauce – ½ cup
- Sugar– ½ cup
- Baking soda– ½ tsp.
- Salt – ½ tsp.

Directions:

In a small bowl, mix together all the dry ingredients. In a large bowl, beat eggs with vanilla, milk, lemon juice, oil, applesauce, and sugar until combined thoroughly. Add dry ingredients into the wet ingredients and stir until combined well. Add chia seeds and fold well. Pour batter into the 12 silicone muffin molds. Place the dehydrating tray into the multi-level air fryer basket and place basket into the instant pot. Place 6 muffin molds on dehydrating tray. Seal pot with air fryer lid. Select bake mode and cook at 350 F for 15 minutes. Cook remaining muffins. Serve.

9-Spinach Tomato Egg Muffins

Cook time: 12 minutes ⎜Serves: 12 ⎜ Per Serving: Calories 57, Carbs 1g, Fat 4g, Protein 5g

Ingredients:

- Eggs – 10
- Spinach – 1 cup, chopped
- Tomatoes – 1 cup, diced
- Italian seasoning – ¾ tsp.
- Garlic powder – ½ tsp.
- Pepper & salt, to taste

Directions:

In a mixing bowl, whisk eggs with garlic powder, Italian seasoning, pepper, and salt. Add spinach and tomatoes and stir well. Pour egg mixture into the 12 silicone muffin molds. Place the dehydrating tray into the multi-level air fryer basket and place basket into the instant pot. Place 6 muffin molds on the dehydrating tray. Seal pot with the air fryer lid. Select bake mode and cook at 380 F for 12 minutes or until set. Cook the remaining muffins. Serve.

10-Breakfast Egg Puffs

Cook time: 15 minutes | Serves: 4 | Per Serving: Calories 105, Carbs 5.3g, Fat 6.2g, Protein 7.5g

Ingredients:

- Eggs – 4
- Taco seasoning – 1 tsp.
- Baking powder – ½ tsp.
- Parmesan cheese – 2 tbsps., grated
- Onion – 2 tbsps., minced
- Bell pepper – 1 tbsp., diced
- Small tomato – 1, diced
- Squash puree – ½ cup
- Cornstarch– 1 tbsp.

Directions:

Spray 4 ramekins with cooking spray and set aside. In a mixing bowl, whisk eggs with remaining ingredients until well combined. Pour egg mixture into the prepared ramekins. Place the dehydrating tray into the multi-level air fryer basket and place basket into the instant pot. Place ramekins on the dehydrating tray. Seal pot with the air fryer lid. Select bake mode and cook at 380 F for 15 minutes or until set. Serve.

11-Easy Spinach Frittata

Cook time: 25 minutes | Serves: 4 | Per Serving: Calories 170, Carbs 5.4g, Fat 11g, Protein 14.2g

Ingredients:

- Spinach – 1 pound, thawed
- Feta cheese – ½ cup, crumbled
- Eggs – 6
- Pepper & salt, to taste

Directions:

In a bowl, whisk eggs with pepper and salt. Add spinach and crumbled cheese and stir well. Pour egg mixture into the baking dish. Place steam rack into the instant pot. Place baking dish on top of the steam rack. Seal pot with air fryer lid. Select bake mode and cook at 350 F for 25 minutes. Serve.

12-Butternut Squash Fritters

Cook time: 20 minutes | Serves: 4 | Per Serving: Calories 151, Carbs 14.3g, Fat 5.8g, Protein 8.9g

Ingredients:

- Butternut squash – 2 cups, shredded
- Dried herbs – ¼ tsp
- Flour – 4 tbsps.
- Dried sage leaves – ½ tsp.
- Parmesan cheese – 2 ½ tbsps., grated
- Eggs – 2, lightly beaten
- Pepper & salt, to taste

Directions:

Add all ingredients into the mixing bowl and mix until well combined. Make small patties from mixture and place into the multi-level air fryer basket and place basket into the instant pot. Seal pot with air fryer lid. Select bake mode and cook at 380 F for 20 minutes. Turn fritters halfway through. Serve.

13-Quick & Easy Frittata

Cook time: 12 minutes | Serves: 4 | Per Serving: Calories 147, Carbs 3g, Fat 11g, Protein 9g

Ingredients:

- Eggs – 4
- Green onion – 2 tbsps., sliced
- Fresh herbs – 2 tbsps., chopped
- Spinach – 4 tbsps., chopped
- Cherry tomatoes – 3, halved
- Mushrooms – 4, sliced
- Cheddar cheese – 4 tbsps, grated
- Heavy cream – 3 tbsps.
- Pepper & salt, to taste

Directions:

In a bowl, whisk eggs, heavy cream, pepper, and salt. Add remaining ingredients and stir well. Pour egg mixture into the baking pan. Place steam rack into the instant pot. Place a baking pan on top of the steam rack. Seal pot with air fryer lid. Select air fry mode and cook at 350 F for 12 minutes. Serve.

14-Breakfast Hash

Cook time: 30 minutes | Serves: 4 | Per Serving: Calories 175, Carbs 23g, Fat 8g, Protein 3g

Ingredients:

- Sweet potato – 1, diced
- Olive oil – 2 tbsps.
- Thyme – 1 tsp.
- Garlic powder – 2 tsps.
- Black pepper – ½ tsp.
- Onion – 1, diced
- Medium potatoes – 2, diced
- Pepper & salt, to taste

Directions:

Add all sweet potatoes and potatoes into the mixing bowl. Add remaining ingredients and toss well. Add sweet potato mixture into the multi-level air fryer basket and place basket into the instant pot. Seal pot with air fryer lid. Select air fry mode and cook at 400 F for 30 minutes. Stir 2-3 times. Serve.

15-Spinach Mushroom Frittata

Cook time: 15 minutes | Serves: 2 | Per Serving: Calories 233, Carbs 6g, Fat 15g, Protein 17g

Ingredients:

- Eggs – 4
- Cheddar cheese – 4 tbsps.
- Bell pepper – 4 tbsps., chopped
- Spinach – ¼ cup, chopped
- Mushrooms – ¼ cup, chopped
- Green onions – 2 tbsps., chopped
- Milk – ½ cup
- Pepper & salt, to taste

Directions:

In a large bowl, whisk eggs with pepper and salt. Add remaining ingredients and stir well. Pour egg mixture into the baking dish. Place steam rack into the instant pot. Place baking dish on top of the steam rack. Seal pot with air fryer lid. Select air fry mode and cook at 360 F for 15 minutes. Serve.

16-Tasty Carrot Fritters

Cook time: 24 minutes | Serves: 5 | Per Serving: Calories 28, Carbs 4.7g, Fat 0.5g, Protein 1.1g

Ingredients:

- Carrot – 1/4 pound, grated
- Ground cumin – ½ tsp.
- Fresh coriander – 2 tbsps., chopped
- All-purpose flour – 4 tbsps.
- Egg – 1, lightly beaten
- Pepper & salt, to taste

Directions:

Add all ingredients into the mixing bowl and mix until well combined. Make small patties from mixture and place into the multi-level air fryer basket and place basket into the instant pot. Seal the pot with the air fryer lid. Select bake mode and cook at 380 F for 24 minutes. Turn fritters halfway through. Serve.

17-Breakfast Sweet Potato Bites

Cook time: 30 minutes | Serves: 2 | Per Serving: Calories 309, Carbs 59.5g, Fat 7.4g, Protein 2.9g

Ingredients:

- Sweet potatoes – 2 ½ cups, chopped
- Cinnamon – 1 tsp.
- Olive oil – 2 tbsps.
- Maple syrup – 2 tbsps.
- Chipotle powder – 1/8 tsp.
- Pepper & salt, to taste

Directions:

Add all ingredients into the mixing bowl and toss well. Add sweet potato mixture into the multi-level air fryer basket and place basket into the instant pot. Seal pot with air fryer lid. Select bake mode and cook at 380 F for 30 minutes. Stir halfway through. Serve.

18-French Toast Sticks

Cook time: 8 minutes | Serves: 3 | Per Serving: Calories 213, Carbs 20g, Fat 12g, Protein 6g

Ingredients:
- Bread slices – 6, cut into slices
- Vanilla – 1/2 tsp.
- Butter – 2 tbsps., melted
- Eggs – 2, lightly beaten
- Milk – 1/2 cup
- Cinnamon – 1/2 tbsp.
- Sugar – 2 tbsps.

Directions:
In a bowl, whisk eggs, vanilla, butter, and milk until well combined. In a separate bowl, mix together sugar and cinnamon. Dip bread slices into the egg mixture and sprinkle with sugar mixture. Place bread slices into the multi-level air fryer basket and place basket into the instant pot. Seal pot with the air fryer lid. Select air fry mode and cook at 350 F for 8 minutes. Serve.

19-Crispy Potatoes

Cook time: 15 minutes | Serves: 2 | Per Serving: Calories 358, Carbs 67g, Fat 7g, Protein 7g

Ingredients:
- Potatoes – 4, peeled and cut into 1-inch pieces
- Paprika – 1/2 tsp.
- Olive oil – 1 tbsp.
- Garlic powder – 1/2 tsp.
- Pepper & salt, to taste

Directions:
Add potatoes into the bowl. Add remaining ingredients and toss until coated thoroughly. Add potatoes into the multi-level air fryer basket and place basket into the instant pot. Seal pot with the air fryer lid. Select air fry mode and cook at 400 F for 15 minutes. Serve.

20-Cheese Sandwich

Cook time: 7 minutes | Serves: 1 | Per Serving: Calories 497, Carbs 11g, Fat 36g, Protein 30g

Ingredients:
- Bread slices – 2
- Cheddar cheese slices – 1
- Butter – 1 tbsp., softened

- Mozzarella cheese slices – 1
- Bacon slices – 2, cooked

Directions:
Spread butter on one side of bread slices. Place one bread slice into the multi-level air fryer basket. Arrange mozzarella cheese slice, bacon slices, and cheddar slice on top of the bread slice. Top with another bread slice. Place air fryer basket into the instant pot. Seal pot with air fryer lid. Select air fry mode and cook at 370 F for 4 minutes. Turn sandwich and air fry for 3 minutes more. Serve.

21-Blueberry Muffins
Cook time: 20 minutes | Serves: 12 | Per Serving: Calories 156, Carbs 12g, Fat 14g, Protein 4g
Ingredients:
- Eggs – 2
- Blueberries – 1/4 cup
- Vanilla – 1/2 tsp.
- Erythritol – 1/2 cup
- Cream cheese – 15 oz
- Almonds, sliced – 1/4 cup

Directions:
Add cream cheese into the mixing bowl and beat until smooth. Add vanilla, eggs, and sweetener and beat until well combined. Add almonds and blueberries and stir well. Pour batter into the 12 silicone muffin molds. Place the dehydrating tray into the multi-level air fryer basket and place basket into the instant pot. Place 6 muffin molds on the dehydrating tray. Seal pot with air fryer lid. Select bake mode and cook at 350 F for 20 minutes or until set. Cook remaining muffins. Serve.

22- Peanut Butter Muffins
Cook time: 16 minutes | Serves: 6 | Per Serving: Calories 186, Carbs 25g, Fat 7g, Protein 6g
Ingredients:
- Egg – 1
- Peanut butter – 1/4 cup
- Sugar – 1/4 cup
- Yogurt – 6 tbsps.
- Rolled oats – 1 cup
- Banana – 1
- Baking soda – 1/4 tsp.
- Baking powder – 1/2 tsp.
- Vanilla – 1/2 tsp.
- Pinch of salt

Directions:
Add all ingredients into the blender and blend until a smooth batter is formed. Pour batter into the 6 silicone muffin molds. Place the dehydrating tray into the multi-

level air fryer basket and place basket into the instant pot. Place muffin molds on the dehydrating tray. Seal pot with the air fryer lid. Select bake mode and cook at 380 F for 16 minutes or until set. Serve.

23- Healthy Oatmeal Muffins

Cook time: 20 minutes │Serves: 6 │ Per Serving: Calories 173, Carbs 26g, Fat 5g, Protein 2g

Ingredients:

- Egg – 1
- Vanilla – 1/2 tsp.
- Ground ginger – 1/4 tsp.
- Ground cinnamon – 1 tsp.
- Baking soda – 1/2 tsp.
- Baking powder – 1/2 tsp.
- Brown sugar – 1/4 cup
- Whole wheat flour – 1/2 cup
- Butter – 2 tbsps., melted
- Applesauce – 1/2 cup
- Milk – 1/4 cup
- Quick oats – 1 cup
- Pinch of salt

Directions:

In a large mixing bowl, mix together all dry ingredients. In a separate bowl, add remaining ingredients and mix well. Add dry ingredient mixture into the wet mixture and mix until combined. Pour batter into the 6 silicone muffin molds. Place the dehydrating tray into the multi-level air fryer basket and place the basket into the instant pot. Place muffin molds on the dehydrating tray. Seal pot with air fryer lid. Select bake mode and cook at 380 F for 20 minutes. Serve.

24- Spicy Jalapeno Egg Muffins

Cook time: 20 minutes │Serves: 12 │ Per Serving: Calories 115, Carbs 1g, Fat 9g, Protein 7g

Ingredients:

- Eggs – 10
- Cream cheese – 1/3 cup
- Jalapeno peppers – 3, chopped
- Onion powder – 1/2 tsp.
- Bacon – 1/3 cup, cooked and crumbled
- Cheddar cheese – 1/2 cup, shredded
- Garlic powder – 1/2 tsp.
- Pepper & salt, to taste

Directions:

In a large bowl, whisk eggs with onion powder, garlic powder, pepper, and salt. Add remaining ingredients and stir well. Pour egg mixture into the 12 silicone muffin molds. Place the dehydrating tray into the multi-level air fryer basket and place the basket into the instant pot. Place 6 muffin molds on the dehydrating tray. Seal pot with the air fryer lid. Select bake mode and cook at 380 F for 20 minutes. Cook remaining muffins. Serve.

25- Greek Breakfast Egg Muffins

Cook time: 20 minutes | Serves: 6 | Per Serving: Calories 69, Carbs 2g, Fat 4g, Protein 6g

Ingredients:

- Eggs – 2
- Egg whites – 4
- Feta cheese – 1/4 cup, crumbled
- Fresh parsley – 1 tbsp., chopped
- Olives – 1/4 cup, diced
- Onion – 1/4 cup, diced
- Tomatoes – 1/4 cup, diced
- Milk – 1/2 cup
- Pepper & salt, to taste

Directions:

In a mixing bowl, whisk eggs, egg whites, milk, pepper, and salt. Add remaining ingredients and stir well. Pour egg mixture into the 6 silicone muffin molds. Place the dehydrating tray into the multi-level air fryer basket and place the basket into the instant pot. Place 6 muffin molds on the dehydrating tray. Seal pot with air fryer lid. Select bake mode and cook at 350 F for 20 minutes. Serve.

SNACKS & APPETIZERS RECIPES

1-Zucchini Crisps

Cook time: 12 minutes | Serves: 2 | Per Serving: Calories 124, Carbs 4g, Fat 7g, Protein 11g

Ingredients:

- Medium zucchini – 1, sliced 1/4–inch thick
- Parmesan cheese – ½ cup, grated
- Olive oil – 1 tbsp.

Directions:

Brush zucchini slices with oil and coat with parmesan cheese. Place zucchini slices into the multi-level air fryer basket and place basket into the instant pot. Seal pot with air fryer lid. Select air fry mode and cook at 370 F for 12 minutes. Serve.

2-Delicious Chickpeas

Cook time: 17 minutes | Serves: 4 | Per Serving: Calories 135, Carbs 25g, Fat 1.4g, Protein 5.6g

Ingredients:

- Can chickpeas – 15 oz, drained
- For seasoning:
- Black pepper – ½ tsp.
- Dry mustard – ½ tsp.
- Garlic powder – ½ tsp.
- Brown sugar – 1 tsp.
- Paprika – 1 ½ tsp.
- Salt – ½ tsp

Directions:

Spread chickpeas in the multi-level air fryer basket and place basket into the instant pot. Seal pot with the air fryer lid. Select air fry mode and cook at 390 F for 17 minutes. Stir halfway through. Once done, then transfer chickpeas into the mixing bowl. Add all seasoning ingredients and toss until well coated. Serve.

3-Crispy Green Beans

Cook time: 5 minutes | Serves: 2 | Per Serving: Calories 195, Carbs 28g, Fat 5g, Protein 10g

Ingredients:

- Green beans – ½ pound, wash & trimmed
- Egg– 1, lightly beaten
- Garlic powder – ¼ tsp.
- Onion powder – 1/4 tsp.
- Parmesan cheese – 2 tbsps., grated
- Breadcrumbs – ½ cup
- Pepper & salt, to taste

Directions:

In a shallow bowl, add the egg. In a separate shallow dish, mix together breadcrumbs, cheese, onion powder, garlic powder, pepper, and salt. Dip green beans in egg and coat with breadcrumb mixture. Place coated green beans into the multi-level air fryer basket and place basket into the instant pot. Seal pot with the air fryer lid. Select air fry mode and cook at 390 F for 5 minutes. Serve.

4-Garlicky Almonds

Cook time: 6 minutes | Serves: 4 | Per Serving: Calories 143, Carbs 6.2g, Fat 11.9g, Protein 5.4g

Ingredients:
- Almonds – 1 cup
- Black pepper – 1/8 tsp.
- Paprika – ½ tsp.
- Garlic powder – ½ tbsp.
- Soy sauce – ½ tbsp.

Directions:
In a bowl, mix together black pepper, paprika, garlic powder, and soy sauce. Add almonds and coat well. Transfer almonds into the multi-level air fryer basket and place basket into the instant pot. Seal pot with the air fryer lid. Select air fry mode and cook at 320 F for 6 minutes. Stir halfway through. Serve.

5-Eggplant Chips

Cook time: 30 minutes | Serves: 2 | Per Serving: Calories 234, Carbs 17g, Fat 11.9g, Protein 17.6g

Ingredients:
- Eggplant – 1, sliced ¼-inch thick
- Fresh rosemary – 2 tbsps., chopped
- Olive oil – 1 tbsp.
- Parmesan cheese – ½ cup, grated
- Pepper & salt, to taste

Directions:
Toss eggplant slices in a mixing bowl with rosemary, oil, parmesan cheese, pepper, and salt. Place eggplant slices into the multi-level air fryer basket and place basket into the instant pot. Seal pot with the air fryer lid. Select air fry mode and cook at 400 F for 30 minutes. Turn eggplant slices halfway through. Serve.

6-Honey Cinnamon Sweet Potato Bites

Cook time: 25 minutes | Serves: 4 | Per Serving: Calories 162, Carbs 34.3g, Fat 3.5g, Protein 1.6g

Ingredients:
- Medium sweet potatoes – 3, peel and diced into cubes
- Cinnamon – 2 tsp.
- Honey – 2 tbsps.
- Olive oil – 1 tbsp.

Directions:

Add sweet potatoes into the mixing bowl. Add remaining ingredients over sweet potatoes and toss well. Add sweet potatoes into the multi-level air fryer basket and place basket into the instant pot. Seal pot with the air fryer lid. Select air fry mode and cook at 400 F for 20-25 minutes. Serve.

7-Healthy Apple Slices
Cook time: 12 minutes │Serves: 1 │ Per Serving: Calories 118, Carbs 31g, Fat 0.5g, Protein 0.5g

Ingredients:
- Apple – 1, core & cut into half-moon slices
- Cinnamon – ¼ tsp.
- Pinch of salt and sugar

Directions:
Sprinkle apple slices with cinnamon, sugar and salt and place into the multi-level air fryer basket and place basket into the instant pot. Seal pot with air fryer lid. Select air fry mode and cook at 390 F for 12 minutes. Turn apple slices halfway through. Serve.

8-Sweet Potato Fries
Cook time: 12 minutes │Serves: 2 │ Per Serving: Calories 149, Carbs 27g, Fat 4g, Protein 2g

Ingredients:
- Medium sweet potatoes – 2, peeled and cut into the shape of fries
- Olive oil – 2 tsp.
- Black pepper – 1/8 tsp.
- Paprika – ¼ tsp.
- Garlic powder – ¼ tsp.
- Salt – ½ tsp.

Directions:
Add sweet potato fries into the mixing bowl and toss with the remaining ingredients. Place sweet potato fries into the multi-level air fryer basket and place basket into the instant pot. Seal pot with the air fryer lid. Select air fry mode and cook at 380 F for 12 minutes. Turn sweet potato fries halfway through. Serve.

9-Zucchini Fritters
Cook time: 12 minutes │Serves: 4 │ Per Serving: Calories 57, Carbs 8g, Fat 1g, Protein 3g

Ingredients:
- Medium zucchini – 2, grated and squeeze out all liquid
- Black pepper – ¼ tsp.
- Paprika – ¼ tsp.
- Onion powder – ¼ tsp.
- Garlic powder – 1 tsp.
- All-purpose flour – 3 tbsps.
- Egg – 1, lightly beaten

- Pepper & salt, to taste

Directions:

Line multi-level air fryer basket with parchment paper and set aside. Add all ingredients into the mixing bowl and mix until well combined. Make small fritters from mixture and place on a parchment paper into the air fryer basket. Place air fryer basket into the instant pot. Seal pot with the air fryer lid. Select air fry mode and cook at 360 F for 12 minutes. Turn fritters halfway through. Serve.

10-Healthy Edamame

Cook time: 18 minutes |Serves: 2 | Per Serving: Calories 191, Carbs 13.5g, Fat 10g, Protein 14.9g

Ingredients:

- Frozen edamame in a shell – 8 oz, defrosted
- Garlic cloves – 2, sliced
- Olive oil – 1 tsp.
- Paprika – ½ tsp.
- Pepper & salt, to taste

Directions:

In a mixing bowl, toss edamame with remaining ingredients. Add edamame into the multi-level air fryer basket and place the basket into the instant pot. Seal pot with the air fryer lid. Select air fry mode and cook at 400 F for 18 minutes. Serve.

11-Crispy Zucchini Fries

Cook time: 15 minutes |Serves: 4 | Per Serving: Calories 237, Carbs 23.7g, Fat 9.3g, Protein 15.1g

Ingredients:

- Zucchini – 1, cut into the shape of fries
- Black pepper – ½ tsp.
- Kosher salt – 1 tsp.
- Garlic powder – 1 tsp.
- Parmesan cheese – ¼ cup, grated
- Breadcrumbs – 1 cup
- Eggs – 2, lightly beaten

Directions:

Add egg in a shallow bowl. In a shallow dish, mix together breadcrumbs, cheese, garlic powder, pepper, and salt. Dip zucchini fries in egg then coat with breadcrumb mixture. Place coated zucchini fries into the multi-level air fryer basket and place basket into the instant pot. Seal pot with the air fryer lid. Select air fry mode and cook at 400 F for 15 minutes. Serve.

12-Roasted Green Beans

Cook time: 8 minutes |Serves: 4 | Per Serving: Calories 59, Carbs 6.6g, Fat 3.6g, Protein 1.7g

Ingredients:

- Green beans – ¾ pound

- Garlic powder – 1 tsp.
- Olive oil – 1 tbsp.
- Pepper & salt, to taste

Directions:

In a mixing bowl, toss green beans with the remaining ingredients. Add green beans into the multi-level air fryer basket and place the basket into the instant pot. Seal pot with the air fryer lid. Select air fry mode and cook at 370 F for 8 minutes. Serve.

13-Crispy Ranch Potatoes

Cook time: 30 minutes | Serves: 4 | Per Serving: Calories 77, Carbs 15g, Fat 1g, Protein 3g

Ingredients:

- Potatoes – 1 pound, cut into chunks
- Dried tarragon – ½ tsp.
- Celery seed – 1/8 tsp.
- Onion powder – ¼ tsp.
- Garlic powder – ½ tsp.
- Dried dill – ¼ tsp.
- Dried parsley – ½ tsp.
- Dried chives – ½ tsp.
- Olive oil– 1 tsp.
- Kosher salt– ½ tsp.

Directions:

In a large bowl, toss potatoes with remaining ingredients until coated thoroughly. Add potatoes into the multi-level air fryer basket and place the basket into the instant pot. Seal pot with the air fryer lid. Select air fry mode and cook at 400 F for 30 minutes. Stir potatoes halfway through. Serve.

14-Healthy Kale Chips

Cook time: 5 minutes | Serves: 1 | Per Serving: Calories 204, Carbs 16.3g, Fat 14.3g, Protein 6.3g

Ingredients:

- Kale – 2 cups
- Nutritional yeast flakes – 1 tbsp.
- Ranch seasoning – 2 tsps.
- Olive oil – 2 tbsps.
- Salt – ¼ tsp.

Directions:

In a large bowl, toss kale with nutritional yeast flakes, ranch seasoning, oil, and salt. Add kale into the multi-level air fryer basket and place the basket into the instant pot. Seal pot with the air fryer lid. Select air fry mode and cook at 370 F for 5 minutes. Stir kale after 2 minutes. Serve.

15-Spicy Roasted Peanuts

Cook time: 20 minutes | Serves: 4 | Per Serving: Calories 191, Carbs 4.6g, Fat 17.5g, Protein 7.3g

Ingredients:

- Peanuts – 4 oz
- Cayenne pepper – ½ tsp.
- Old bay seasoning – 1 ½ tsps.
- Olive oil – 1 tbsp.
- Salt, to taste

Directions:

In a mixing bowl, mix together the cayenne pepper, old bay seasoning, olive oil, and salt. Add peanuts and stir until coated thoroughly. Transfer peanuts into the multi-level air fryer basket and place basket into the instant pot. Seal the pot with the air fryer lid. Select air fry mode and cook at 320 F for 20 minutes. Stir peanuts after 10 minutes. Serve.

16- Roasted Cashew Nuts

Cook time: 5 minutes | Serves: 6 | Per Serving: Calories 435, Carbs 22g, Fat 36g, Protein 10g

Ingredients:

- Cashews – 3 cups
- Ground coriander – 1 tsp.
- Paprika – 1 tsp.
- Olive oil – 2 tbsps.
- Ground cumin – 1 tsp.
- Salt – 1 tsp.

Directions:

Add cashews and remaining ingredients into the large bowl and toss well. Add cashews into the multi-level air fryer basket and place the basket into the instant pot. Seal pot with the air fryer lid. Select air fry mode and cook at 330 F for 5 minutes. Serve.

17- Easy Potato Wedges

Cook time: 24 minutes | Serves: 2 | Per Serving: Calories 135, Carbs 17g, Fat 7g, Protein 2g

Ingredients:

- Potatoes – 1/2 pound, cut into wedges
- Olive oil – 1 tbsp.
- Paprika – 1/4 tsp.
- Pepper & salt, to taste

Directions:

In a bowl, toss potato wedges with oil, paprika, pepper, and salt. Add potato wedges into the multi-level air fryer basket and place the basket into the instant pot. Seal pot with the air fryer lid. Select air fry mode and cook at 390 F for 24 minutes. Stir halfway through. Serve.

18- Sweet Potato Wedges

Cook time: 20 minutes | Serves: 2 | Per Serving: Calories 175, Carbs 24g, Fat 8g, Protein 2g

Ingredients:

- Sweet potatoes – 2, cut into wedges
- Ground cumin – 1 tsp.
- Olive oil – 1 tbsp.
- Chili powder – 1 tsp.
- Mustard powder – 1 tsp.
- Pepper & salt, to taste

Directions:

Add sweet potato wedges into the mixing bowl and toss with the remaining ingredients. Add sweet potato wedges into the multi-level air fryer basket and place basket into the instant pot. Seal pot with the air fryer lid. Select air fry mode and cook at 350 F for 20 minutes. Stir halfway through. Serve.

19- Healthy Spinach Balls

Cook time: 25 minutes | Serves: 6 | Per Serving: Calories 185, Carbs 15g, Fat 11g, Protein 6g

Ingredients:

- Eggs – 3, lightly beaten
- Onion – 1/2, chopped
- Breadcrumb – 1 cup
- Frozen spinach – 6 oz, thawed
- Butter – 1/4 cup, melted
- Mozzarella cheese – 1/4 cup, shredded
- Pepper & salt, to taste

Directions:

Add all ingredients into the mixing bowl and mix until combined thoroughly. Make small balls from the mixture and place into the multi-level air fryer basket and then place the basket into the instant pot. Seal pot with the air fryer lid. Select bake mode and cook at 350 F for 25 minutes. Serve.

20- Delicious Jalapeno Poppers

Cook time: 8 minutes | Serves: 4 | Per Serving: Calories 265, Carbs 13g, Fat 20g, Protein 6g

Ingredients:

- Jalapeno pepper – 10, halved and remove seeds
- Cream cheese – 8 oz
- Garlic powder – 1/4 tsp.
- Breadcrumbs – 1/2 cup
- Parsley – 1/4 cup, chopped

Directions:

Mix together cream cheese, breadcrumbs, parsley, and garlic powder in a bowl. Stuff cheese mixture into each jalapeno half. Place stuffed jalapeno halves into the multi-level air fryer basket and place basket into the instant pot. Seal the pot with the air fryer lid. Select air fry mode and cook at 370 F for 8 minutes. Serve.

21- Spicy Chickpeas
Cook time: 12 minutes | Serves: 4 | Per Serving: Calories 195, Carbs 27g, Fat 7g, Protein 6g

Ingredients:
- Can chickpeas – 2 cups, drained and rinsed
- Chili powder – 1 tsp.
- Butter – 2 tbsps., melted
- Ground coriander – 1 tsp.
- Pepper & salt, to taste

Directions:
Add all ingredients into the mixing bowl and toss well. Add chickpeas into the multi-level air fryer basket and place basket into the instant pot. Seal pot with air fryer lid. Select air fry mode and cook at 400 F for 12 minutes. Serve.

22- Sausage Balls
Cook time: 15 minutes | Serves: 8 | Per Serving: Calories 48, Carbs 2g, Fat 2g, Protein 2g

Ingredients:
- Ground sausage meat – 4 oz
- Garlic – 1/2 tsp., minced
- Sage – 1 tsp.
- Breadcrumbs – 3 tbsps.
- Small onion – 1, chopped
- Pepper & salt, to taste

Directions:
Add all ingredients into the mixing bowl and mix until combined well. Make small balls from the meat mixture and place it into the multi-level air fryer basket and place basket into the instant pot. Seal pot with air fryer lid. Select air fry mode and cook at 360 F for 15 minutes. Serve.

23- Tofu Bites
Cook time: 20 minutes | Serves: 4 | Per Serving: Calories 84, Carbs 2g, Fat 6g, Protein 7g

Ingredients:
- Tofu – 12 oz, cubed
- Dried rosemary – 1 1/2 tsps.
- Vinegar – 1 tsp.
- Olive oil – 2 tsps.
- Pepper & salt, to taste

Directions:
Add all ingredients into the bowl and toss well. Transfer tofu into the multi-level air fryer basket and place the basket into the instant pot. Seal pot with the air fryer lid.

Select air fry mode and cook at 350 F for 20 minutes. Turn tofu pieces halfway through. Serve.

24- Beet Chips

Cook time: 30 minutes │Serves: 2 │ Per Serving: Calories 42, Carbs 5g, Fat 2g, Protein 1g

Ingredients:

- Medium beet – 1, peeled and sliced thinly
- Olive oil – 1 tsp.
- Pepper & salt, to taste

Directions:

Add sliced beets, oil, pepper, and salt into the bowl and toss well. Place beet slices into the multi-level air fryer basket and place basket into the instant pot. Seal pot with the air fryer lid. Select air fry mode and cook at 320 F for 30 minutes. Turn beet slices halfway through. Serve.

25- Tasty Cajun Zucchini Chips

Cook time: 16 minutes │Serves: 2 │ Per Serving: Calories 75, Carbs 3g, Fat 7g, Protein 1g

Ingredients:

- Zucchini – 1, cut into 1/8-inch thick slices
- Cajun seasoning – 1 tsp.
- Olive oil – 1 tbsp.
- Pepper & salt, to taste

Directions:

Add zucchini slices into the mixing bowl and toss with the remaining ingredients. Place zucchini slices into the multi-level air fryer basket and place the basket into the instant pot. Seal pot with the air fryer lid. Select air fry mode and cook at 370 F for 16 minutes. Turn zucchini slices halfway through. Serve.

SOUP RECIPES

1-Cauliflower Soup

Cook time: 25 minutes | Serves: 6 | Per Serving: Calories 330, Carbs 9g, Fat 24g, Protein 19g

Ingredients:

- Medium cauliflower head – 1, cut into florets
- Vegetable broth – 3 cups
- Garlic – 1 tsp., minced
- Celery stalk – 1, chopped
- Onion – 1, chopped
- Olive oil – 1 tbsp.
- Pepper & salt, to taste
- Cheddar cheese – 1 1/2 cups, shredded
- Sour cream – 1/2 cup
- For Croutons:
- Cornbread cubes – 1 1/2 cups
- Olive oil –2 tbsps.
- Pepper & salt, to taste

Directions:

Add oil into the instant pot and set the pot on sauté mode. Add garlic, celery, onion, pepper, and salt and sauté for 5 minutes. Add cauliflower and broth and stir well. Seal pot with the pressure-cooking lid and cook on high for 5 minutes. Release pressure using quick release. Remove lid. Add 1 cup of shredded cheese and sour cream and stir well. Puree the soup using a blender until smooth.

For Croutons:

In a bowl, toss bread cubes with the remaining ingredients. Add cornbread cubes into the multi-level air fryer basket and place the basket into the instant pot. Seal pot with the air fryer lid. Select bake mode and cook at 350 F for 15 minutes. Stir halfway through. Top soup with remaining cheese and croutons and serve.

2-Healthy Asparagus Broccoli Soup

Cook time: 18 minutes | Serves: 6 | Per Serving: Calories 172, Carbs 13g, Fat 10g, Protein 9g

Ingredients:

- Asparagus spears – 15, cut the ends and chopped
- Cauliflower florets – 2 cups
- Broccoli florets – 2 cups
- Garlic – 2 tsp., chopped
- Onion – 1 cup, chopped
- Dried mixed herbs – 1 tsp.
- Nutritional yeast – 1/4 cup
- Coconut milk – 1/2 cup

- Vegetable broth – 3 1/2 cups
- Olive oil – 2 tbsps.
- Pepper & salt, to taste
- For Croutons:
- Bread cubes – 2 cups
- Garlic powder – 1/4 tsp.
- Dried parsley – 1/2 tsp.
- Dried thyme – 1/8 tsp.
- Dried oregano – 1/4 tsp.
- Parmesan cheese – 1 tbsp., grated
- Olive oil – 1 tbsp.
- Pepper & salt, to taste

Directions:
Add oil into the instant pot and set the pot on sauté mode. Add onion and garlic and sauté for 5 minutes. Add broth and all vegetables and stir well. Seal pot with the pressure-cooking lid and cook on high for 3 minutes. Allow to release pressure naturally. Remove lid. Puree the soup using a blender until smooth. Add coconut milk, nutritional yeast, herbs, pepper, and salt and stir well.
For Croutons:
In a bowl, toss bread cubes with the remaining ingredients. Add bread cubes into the multi-level air fryer basket and place the basket into the instant pot. Seal pot with the air fryer lid. Select bake mode and cook at 375 F for 10 minutes. Stir halfway through. Top soup with croutons and serve.

3-Creamy Asparagus Soup

Cook time: 17 minutes ┃Serves: 4 ┃ Per Serving: Calories 41, Carbs 6g, Fat 2g, Protein 2g
Ingredients:
- Asparagus – 12 oz, trimmed and chopped
- Vegetable stock – 2 1/2 cups
- Garlic – 1 tsp., chopped
- Small onion – 1 tsp., chopped
- Olive oil – 1 tsp.
- Nutritional yeast – 1 tsp.
- Fresh lemon juice – 2 tsps.
- Lemon zest – 1/4 tsp.
- Dried mint – 1/4 tsp.
- Pepper & salt, to taste
- For Croutons:
- Croissant – 1, cut into 1/2-inch cubes
- Dried oregano – 1/2 tsp.
- Parmesan cheese – 2 tbsps., grated

- Olive oil – 1 tbsp.
- Pepper & salt, to taste

Directions:

Add oil into the instant pot and set the pot on sauté mode. Add garlic and onion and sauté for 2 minutes. Add asparagus, lemon zest, mint, pepper, and salt and sauté for a minute. Add stock and stir well. Seal pot with the pressure-cooking lid and cook on high for 3 minutes. Release pressure using quick release. Remove lid. Puree the soup using a blender until smooth. Add nutritional yeast and lemon juice and stir well.

For Croutons:

In a bowl, toss bread cubes with the remaining ingredients. Add bread cubes into the multi-level air fryer basket and place the basket into the instant pot. Seal pot with the air fryer lid. Select bake mode and cook at 350 F for 10 minutes. Stir halfway through. Top soup with croutons and serve.

4-Leek Mushroom Soup

Cook time: 20 minutes │Serves: 4 │ Per Serving: Calories 102, Carbs 6g, Fat 8g, Protein 2g

Ingredients:

- Mushrooms – 2 cups, chopped
- Dried parsley – 1 tsp.
- Leeks – 1 cup, chopped
- Garlic cloves – 2, chopped
- Olive oil – 1 tbsp.
- Coconut milk – 1/3 cup
- Vegetable stock – 1 cup
- White pepper powder – 1 tsp.
- For Croutons:
- Bread cubes – 2 cups
- Olive oil – 1 tbsp.
- Dried rosemary – 1/2 tsp.
- Garlic powder – 1/2 tsp.
- Pepper & salt, to taste

Directions:

Add oil into the instant pot and set the pot on sauté mode. Add garlic and sauté for 30 seconds. Add leek and mushrooms and sauté for 2 minutes. Add remaining ingredients except for coconut milk and stir well. Seal pot with the pressure-cooking lid and cook on high for 2 minutes. Allow to release pressure naturally. Remove lid. Puree the soup using a blender until smooth. Add coconut milk and stir well.

For Croutons:

In a bowl, toss bread cubes with remaining ingredients. Add bread cubes into the multi-level air fryer basket and place the basket into the instant pot. Seal pot with the air fryer lid. Select bake mode and cook at 350 F for 15 minutes. Stir halfway through. Top soup with croutons and serve.

5-Delicious Pumpkin Soup

Cook time: 35 minutes | Serves: 6 | Per Serving: Calories 166, Carbs 10g, Fat 12g, Protein 3g

Ingredients:

- Can pumpkin puree – 15 oz
- Garlic –, 1 tsp. sliced
- Ginger –, 2 tsps. grated
- Small onion –, 1 chopped
- Olive oil – 1 tbsp.
- Coconut milk – 1 cup
- Vegetable broth – 2 cups
- Nutmeg – 1/2 tsp.
- Pepper & salt, to taste
- For Croutons:
- Bread cubes – 2 cups
- Parmesan cheese – 2 tbsps, grated
- Butter – 2 tbsps., melted
- Garlic clove – 1, minced
- Olive oil – 1 tbsp.
- Pepper & salt, to taste

Directions:

Add oil into the instant pot and set the pot on sauté mode. Add onion and sauté until softened. Add ginger and garlic and sauté for 30 seconds. Add remaining ingredients except for coconut milk and stir well. Seal pot with the pressure-cooking lid and cook on high for 5 minutes. Release pressure using quick release. Remove lid. Puree the soup using a blender until smooth. Add coconut milk and stir well.

For Croutons:

In a bowl, toss bread cubes with butter, garlic, oil, pepper, and salt. Add bread cubes into the multi-level air fryer basket and place basket into the instant pot. Seal pot with the air fryer lid. Select bake mode and cook at 375 F for 15 minutes. Stir halfway through. Toss bread cubes with parmesan cheese. Top soup with croutons and serve.

6-Tomato Basil Soup

Cook time: 55 minutes | Serves: 6 | Per Serving: Calories 299, Carbs 13g, Fat 25g, Protein 7g

Ingredients:

- Can tomatoes – 28 oz
- Romano cheese – 1/3 cup, grated
- Coconut milk – 1 3/4 cups
- Chicken stock – 3 1/2 cups
- Onion – 1 cup, diced
- Celery – 1 cup, diced
- Bay leaf – 1

- Fresh basil – 1/2 cup, chopped
- Fresh thyme sprig – 1
- Carrots – 2, diced
- Butter – 1 tbsp.
- Olive oil – 2 tbsps.
- Pepper & salt, to taste
- For Croutons:
- Cornbread cubes – 1 1/2 cups
- Olive oil –2 tbsps.
- Pepper & salt, to taste

Directions:

Add oil and butter into the instant pot and set the pot on sauté mode. Add celery, onion, and carrots and sauté for 5 minutes. Add remaining ingredients and stir well. Seal pot with the pressure cooking lid and cook on high for 30 minutes. Release pressure using quick release. Remove lid. Puree the soup using an immersion blender until smooth.

For Croutons:

In a bowl, toss bread cubes with remaining ingredients. Add cornbread cubes into the multi-level air fryer basket and place the basket into the instant pot. Seal pot with the air fryer lid. Select bake mode and cook at 350 F for 15 minutes. Stir halfway through. Top soup with the remaining cheese and croutons and serve.

7-Creamy Zucchini Soup

Cook time: 12 minutes │Serves: 2 │ Per Serving: Calories 316, Carbs 15g, Fat 29g, Protein 5g

Ingredients:

- Zucchini – 2, chopped
- Garlic powder – 1/2 tsp.
- Coconut milk – 1 cup
- Curry powder – 1 tsp.
- Onion powder – 3/4 tsp.
- Water – 1 cup
- Pepper & salt, to taste
- For Croutons:
- Bread cubes – 2 cups
- Garlic powder – 1/4 tsp.
- Dried parsley – 1/2 tsp.
- Dried thyme – 1/8 tsp.
- Dried oregano – 1/4 tsp.
- Parmesan cheese – 1 tbsp., grated
- Olive oil – 1 tbsp.
- Pepper & salt, to taste

Directions:

Pour water into the instant pot then place steamer rack in the pot. Arrange zucchini on top of the steamer rack. Seal pot with the pressure-cooking lid and cook on high for 2 minutes. Release pressure using quick release. Remove lid. Transfer zucchini into the blender along with remaining ingredients and blend until smooth.

For Croutons:

In a bowl, toss bread cubes with remaining ingredients. Add bread cubes into the multi-level air fryer basket and place the basket into the instant pot. Seal pot with the air fryer lid. Select bake mode and cook at 375 F for 10 minutes. Stir halfway through. Top soup with croutons and serve.

8-Healthy Carrot Soup

Cook time: 22 minutes | Serves: 4 | Per Serving: Calories 378, Carbs 25g, Fat 28g, Protein 8g

Ingredients:

- Carrots – 5, peeled and chopped
- Vegetable broth – 4 cups
- Ginger – 2 tbsps., chopped
- Garlic – 1 tsp., minced
- Onion – 1, chopped
- Fresh lime juice – 1 tbsp.
- Can coconut milk – 14 oz
- Dried thyme – 1 tsp.
- Olive oil – 1 tbsp.
- Pepper & salt, to taste
- For Croutons:
- Croissant – 1, cut into 1/2-inch cubes
- Dried oregano – 1/2 tsp.
- Parmesan cheese – 2 tbsps., grated
- Olive oil – 1 tbsp.
- Pepper & salt, to taste

Directions:

Add oil into the instant pot and set the pot on sauté mode. Add onion and sauté for 5 minutes. Add ginger and garlic and cook for 2 minutes. Add remaining ingredients except for coconut milk and lime juice and stir well. Seal pot with the pressure-cooking lid and cook on high for 5 minutes. Release pressure using the quick release. Remove lid. Puree the soup using a blender until smooth. Add lime juice and coconut milk and stir well.

For Croutons:

In a bowl, toss bread cubes with the remaining ingredients. Add bread cubes into the multi-level air fryer basket and place the basket into the instant pot. Seal pot with the air fryer lid. Select bake mode and cook at 350 F for 10 minutes. Stir halfway through. Top soup with croutons and serve.

9-Creamy Tomato Soup

Cook time: 50 minutes | Serves: 6 | Per Serving: Calories 296, Carbs 15g, Fat 25g, Protein 5g

Ingredients:

- Can tomatoes – 28 oz
- Coconut milk – 1 3/4 cups
- Fresh basil – 1/2 cup, chopped
- Fresh thyme sprig – 1
- Carrots – 1 cup, diced
- Celery – 1 cup, diced
- Chicken stock – 3 1/2 cups
- Onion – 1 cup, diced
- Cheddar cheese – 1/3 cup, grated
- Bay leaves – 2
- Butter – 1 tbsp.
- Olive oil – 2 tbsps.
- Pepper & salt, to taste
- For Croutons:
- Bread cubes – 2 cups
- Olive oil – 1 tbsp.
- Dried rosemary – 1/2 tsp.
- Garlic powder – 1/2 tsp.
- Pepper & salt, to taste

Directions:

Add olive oil and butter into the pot and set the pot on sauté mode. Add celery, onion, and carrots and sauté for 5 minutes. Add remaining ingredients and stir well. Seal pot with the pressure-cooking lid and cook on high for 30 minutes. Release pressure using the quick-release method. Remove the lid. Puree the soup using a blender until smooth.

For Croutons:

In a bowl, toss bread cubes with the remaining ingredients. Add bread cubes into the multi-level air fryer basket and place the basket into the instant pot. Seal pot with air fryer lid. Select bake mode and cook at 350 F for 15 minutes. Stir halfway through. Top soup with croutons and serve.

10-Creamy Squash Soup

Cook time: 25 minutes | Serves: 6 | Per Serving: Calories 134, Carbs 18g, Fat 7g, Protein 2g

Ingredients:

- Butternut squash – 6 cups, peeled and cubed
- Olive oil – 2 tbsps.
- Cayenne pepper – 1/8 tsp.
- Thyme – 2 tsp.
- Nutmeg – 1/8 tsp.

- Chicken stock – 3 cups
- Onion – 1, chopped
- Heavy cream – 1/4 cup
- Pepper & salt, to taste
- For Croutons:
- Bread cubes – 2 cups
- Parmesan cheese – 2 tbsps., grated
- Butter – 2 tbsps., melted
- Garlic clove – 1, minced
- Olive oil – 1 tbsp.
- Pepper & salt, to taste

Directions:

Add oil into the instant pot and set the pot on sauté mode. Add onion to the pot and sauté for 3 minutes. Add squash, nutmeg, cayenne, thyme, stock, and salt. Stir well. Seal pot with the pressure-cooking lid and cook on high for 5 minutes. Allow to release pressure naturally. Remove lid. Add heavy cream and stir well. Puree the soup using a blender until smooth. Season soup with pepper and salt

For Croutons:

In a bowl, toss bread cubes with butter, garlic, oil, pepper, and salt. Add bread cubes into the multi-level air fryer basket and place basket into the instant pot. Seal pot with the air fryer lid. Select bake mode and cook at 375 F for 15 minutes. Stir halfway through. Toss bread cubes with parmesan cheese. Top soup with croutons and serve.

VEGETARIAN RECIPES

1-Cauliflower Bites
Cook time: 16 minutes │Serves: 4 │ Per Serving: Calories 106, Carbs 6g, Fat 9g, Protein 2g
Ingredients:

- Cauliflower head – 1, cut into florets
- Old bay seasoning – ½ tsp.
- Paprika – ¼ tsp.
- Garlic – 1 tbsp., minced
- Olive oil – 3 tbsps.
- Pepper & salt, to taste

Directions:
Add cauliflower florets into the large bowl. Add remaining ingredients and toss well. Add cauliflower florets into the multi-level air fryer basket and place basket into the instant pot. Seal pot with the air fryer lid. Select air fry mode and cook at 400 F for 16 minutes. Turn cauliflower florets halfway through. Serve.

2-Healthy Broccoli Bites
Cook time: 5 minutes │Serves: 2 │ Per Serving: Calories 176, Carbs 7g, Fat 14g, Protein 3g
Ingredients:

- Broccoli florets – 4 cups
- Olive oil – 2 tbsps.
- Nutritional yeast – 1 tbsp.
- Pepper & salt, to taste

Directions:
Add broccoli florets and remaining ingredients into the mixing bowl and toss well. Add broccoli florets into the multi-level air fryer basket and place basket into the instant pot. Seal pot with the air fryer lid. Select air fry mode and cook at 370 F for 5 minutes. Serve.

3-Asparagus with Almonds
Cook time: 5 minutes │Serves: 4 │ Per Serving: Calories 135, Carbs 8g, Fat 11g, Protein 3g
Ingredients:

- Asparagus spears – 16, trimmed
- Olive oil – 2 tbsps.
- Balsamic vinegar – 2 tbsps.
- Sliced almonds – 1/3 cup
- Pepper & salt, to taste

Directions:
In a bowl, toss asparagus with oil and balsamic vinegar. Add asparagus spears into the multi-level air fryer basket. Sprinkle sliced almonds on top of asparagus. Place

the basket into the instant pot. Seal pot with air fryer lid. Select air fry mode and cook at 350 F for 5 minutes. Serve.

4-Sesame Carrots

Cook time: 14 minutes │Serves: 4 │ Per Serving: Calories 101, Carbs 9g, Fat 7g, Protein 2g

Ingredients:

- Sliced carrots – 2 cups
- Sesame seeds – 1 tsp.
- Green onion – 1 tbsp.
- Garlic – 1 tsp., minced
- Soy sauce – 1 tbsp.
- Ginger – 1 tbsp., minced
- Sesame oil – 2 tbsps.

Directions:

In a mixing bowl, add all ingredients, except green onion and sesame seeds. Pour carrot mixture into the multi-level air fryer basket and place the basket into the instant pot. Seal pot with the air fryer lid. Select air fry mode and cook at 375 F for 14 minutes. Stir halfway through. Garnish with green onion and sesame seeds. Serve.

5-Perfect Zucchini & Squash

Cook time: 20 minutes │Serves: 4 │ Per Serving: Calories 56, Carbs 8.2g, Fat 2.5g, Protein 2.1g

Ingredients:

- Zucchini – 1 pound, cut into ½-inch half-moons
- Yellow squash – 1 pound, cut into ½-inch half-moons
- Olive oil – 2 tsps.
- Pepper & salt, to taste

Directions:

Add zucchini and squash into the mixing bowl. Add oil, pepper, and salt and toss well. Transfer zucchini and squash into the multi-level air fryer basket and place basket into the instant pot. Seal pot with the air fryer lid. Select air fry mode and cook at 400 F for 20 minutes. Stir halfway through. Serve.

6-Roasted Carrots

Cook time: 20 minutes │Serves: 2 │ Per Serving: Calories 121, Carbs 15g, Fat 7g, Protein 1g

Ingredients:

- Baby carrots – 8 oz
- Olive oil – 1 tbsp.
- Brown sugar – 1 tbsp.
- Pepper & salt, to taste

Directions:

In a mixing bowl, toss baby carrots with remaining ingredients. Add baby carrots into the multi-level air fryer basket and place basket into the instant pot. Seal pot with the air fryer lid. Select air fry mode and cook at 360 F for 20 minutes. Stir halfway through. Serve.

7-Healthy Brussels Sprouts & Sweet Potatoes

Cook time: 16 minutes | Serves: 6 | Per Serving: Calories 179, Carbs 22g, Fat 9g, Protein 4g

Ingredients:

- Brussels sprouts – 1 pound, cut in half
- Sweet potatoes – 1 pound, cut into ½-inch cubes
- Black pepper – ½ tsp.
- Chili powder – 1 tsp.
- Olive oil – 4 tbsps.
- Pepper & salt, to taste

Directions:

Add sweet potatoes and Brussels sprouts into the mixing bowl. Add remaining ingredients and toss well. Transfer sweet potatoes and Brussels sprouts mixture into the multi-level air fryer basket and place the basket into the instant pot. Seal pot with the air fryer lid. Select air fry mode and cook at 380 F for 16 minutes. Stir halfway through. Serve.

8-Parmesan Brussels Sprouts

Cook time: 12 minutes | Serves: 4 | Per Serving: Calories 155, Carbs 6g, Fat 13g, Protein 6g

Ingredients:

- Brussels sprouts – 2 cups, cut in half
- Bagel seasoning – 2 tbsps.
- Sliced almonds – 4 tbsps.
- Grated parmesan cheese – 4 tbsps.
- Olive oil – 2 tbsps.
- Pepper & salt, to taste

Directions:

Add 2 cups of water and Brussels sprouts into the saucepan and cook over medium heat for 10 minutes. Drain Brussels sprouts well and place in a mixing bowl. Add the remaining ingredients over the Brussels sprouts and toss well. Transfer Brussels sprouts mixture into the multi-level air fryer basket and place basket into the instant pot. Seal pot with air fryer lid. Select air fry mode and cook at 375 F for 12 minutes. Stir halfway through. Serve.

9-Flavorful Cauliflower

Cook time: 20 minutes | Serves: 4 | Per Serving: Calories 91, Carbs 6g, Fat 7g, Protein 2g

Ingredients:

- Cauliflower florets – 4 cups
- Ground cumin – 1 tsp.
- Olive oil – 2 tbsps.

- Garlic cloves – 2, minced
- Pepper & salt, to taste

Directions:

Toss cauliflower florets with remaining ingredients into the bowl. Transfer cauliflower florets into the multi-level air fryer basket and place basket into the instant pot. Seal pot with the air fryer lid. Select air fry mode and cook at 400 F for 20 minutes. Stir halfway through. Serve.

10-Quick & Easy Green Beans

Cook time: 10 minutes |Serves: 2 | Per Serving: Calories 158, Carbs 8g, Fat 14g, Protein 2g

Ingredients:

- Green beans – 2 cups
- Olive oil – 2 tbsps.
- Shawarma spice mix – 1 tbsp.
- Pepper & salt, to taste

Directions:

Toss green beans with shawarma spice, oil, and salt. Place green beans into the multi-level air fryer basket and place the basket into the instant pot. Seal pot with the air fryer lid. Select air fry mode and cook at 370 F for 10 minutes. Turn green beans halfway through. Serve.

11-Roasted Rosemary Potatoes

Cook time: 16 minutes |Serves: 4 | Per Serving: Calories 212, Carbs 27g, Fat 10g, Protein 3g

Ingredients:

- Baby potatoes – 4 cups, cut into chunks
- Olive oil – 3 tbsps.
- Fresh parsley – 4 tbsps., chopped
- Lime juice – 1 tbsp.
- Garlic – 1 tbsp., minced
- Dried rosemary – 2 tsps., minced
- Pepper & salt, to taste

Directions:

Add potatoes and remaining ingredients into the mixing bowl and toss well. Transfer potatoes into the multi-level air fryer basket and place the basket into the instant pot. Seal pot with the air fryer lid. Select air fry mode and cook at 400 F for 16 minutes. Stir halfway through. Serve.

12-Asian Butternut Squash

Cook time: 15 minutes |Serves: 4 | Per Serving: Calories 128, Carbs 16g, Fat 7g, Protein 1g

Ingredients:

- Butternut squash – 4 cups, cut into 1-inch cubes
- Olive oil – 2 tbsps.

- Brown sugar – 1 tbsp.
- Chinese 5 spice powder – 1 tsp.

Directions:

In a mixing bowl, toss butternut squash with the remaining ingredients. Add butternut squash into the multi-level air fryer basket and place the basket into the instant pot. Seal pot with the air fryer lid. Select air fry mode and cook at 400 F for 15 minutes. Stir halfway through. Serve.

13- Healthy Baked Okra

Cook time: 15 minutes | Serves: 4 | Per Serving: Calories 107, Carbs 8g, Fat 7g, Protein 2g

Ingredients:

- Okra –1 pound, cut into 3/4-inch pieces
- Paprika – 1 tsp.
- Chili powder – 1/4 tsp.
- Olive oil – 2 tbsps.
- Pepper & salt, to taste

Directions:

Add okra, chili powder, paprika, oil, and salt into the mixing bowl and toss well. Add okra into the multi-level air fryer basket and place basket into the instant pot. Seal pot with the air fryer lid. Select bake mode and cook at 380 F for 15 minutes. Serve.

14- Potato Carrot Roast

Cook time: 40 minutes | Serves: 2 | Per Serving: Calories 199, Carbs 31g, Fat 7g, Protein 3g

Ingredients:

- Potatoes – 1/2 pound, cut into 1-inch cubes
- Carrots – 1/2 pound, peeled & cut into chunks
- Italian seasoning – 1/2 tsp.
- Olive oil – 1 tbsp.
- Onion – 1/2, diced
- Pepper & salt, to taste

Directions:

In a mixing bowl, toss carrots, potatoes, Italian seasoning, oil, onion, pepper, and salt. Transfer carrot potato mixture into the multi-level air fryer basket and place the basket into the instant pot. Seal pot with the air fryer lid. Select roast mode and cook at 380 F for 40 minutes. Stir twice. Serve.

15- Baked Mushrooms

Cook time: 15 minutes | Serves: 4 | Per Serving: Calories 57, Carbs 4g, Fat 3g, Protein 3g

Ingredients:

- Mushrooms – 1 pound, clean & stems trimmed
- Garlic cloves – 2, chopped
- Olive oil – 1 tbsp.

- Garlic powder – 1/8 tsp.
- Chives – 2 tbsps., chopped
- Pepper & salt, to taste

Directions:

Add mushrooms into the bowl. Add remaining ingredients and toss well. Add mushrooms into the multi-level air fryer basket and place the basket into the instant pot. Seal pot with the air fryer lid. Select bake mode and cook at 380 F for 15 minutes. Serve.

16- Healthy Mixed Vegetable

Cook time: 30 minutes | Serves: 6 | Per Serving: Calories 154, Carbs 18g, Fat 8g, Protein 2g

Ingredients:

- Potatoes – 1 pound, cut into 1/8-inch thick slices
- Carrots – 2, sliced
- Onion – 1, sliced
- Dried tarragon – 1 tsp.
- Zucchini – 1, sliced
- Bell pepper – 1, sliced
- Dried thyme – 1 tsp.
- Garlic – 2 tsps., chopped
- Olive oil – 4 tbsps.
- Pepper & salt, to taste

Directions:

Add all ingredients into the mixing bowl and toss well. Pour vegetable mixture into the multi-level air fryer basket and place basket into the instant pot. Seal pot with the air fryer lid. Select bake mode and cook at 380 F for 30 minutes. Stir halfway through. Serve.

17-Cheesy Broccoli Bites

Cook time: 30 minutes | Serves: 6 | Per Serving: Calories 89, Carbs 7g, Fat 4g, Protein 5g

Ingredients:

- Broccoli head – 3 cups, boil and chopped finely
- Cheddar cheese – 1/2 cup, shredded
- Breadcrumbs – 1/2 cup
- Egg – 1, lightly beaten
- Pepper & salt, to taste

Directions:

Add all ingredients into the mixing bowl and mix until well combined. Make small balls from the broccoli mixture and place them into the multi-level air fryer basket and place the basket into the instant pot. Seal pot with the air fryer lid. Select bake mode and cook at 350 F for 30 minutes. Turn halfway through. Serve.

18- Delicious Broccoli Fritters

Cook time: 30 minutes | Serves: 4 | Per Serving: Calories 326, Carbs 7g, Fat 24g, Protein 20g

Ingredients:

- Broccoli florets – 3 cups, steam & chopped
- Eggs – 2, lightly beaten
- Garlic – 1 tsp., minced
- Cheddar cheese – 2 cups, shredded
- Almond flour – 1/4 cup
- Pepper & salt, to taste

Directions:

Add all ingredients into the bowl and mix until well combined. Make patties from the broccoli mixture and place it into the multi-level air fryer basket and place the basket into the instant pot. Seal pot with the air fryer lid. Select bake mode and cook at 375 F for 30 minutes. Turn patties halfway through. Serve.

19- Easy Parmesan Cauliflower

Cook time: 30 minutes | Serves: 2 | Per Serving: Calories 70, Carbs 4g, Fat 5g, Protein 3g

Ingredients:

- Cauliflower head – 1/2 pound, cut into florets
- Garlic – 1/2 tbsp., minced
- Olive oil – 1/2 tbsp.
- Parmesan cheese – 1/4 cup, grated
- Paprika –1/2 tsp.
- Pepper & salt, to taste

Directions:

Add all ingredients except cheese into the mixing bowl and toss well. Add cauliflower mixture into the multi-level air fryer basket and place the basket into the instant pot. Seal pot with the air fryer lid. Select bake mode and cook at 380 F for 15 minutes. Sprinkle parmesan cheese on top of the cauliflower florets and bake for 15 minutes more. Serve.

20- Honey Dill Carrots

Cook time: 12 minutes | Serves: 2 | Per Serving: Calories 85, Carbs 13g, Fat 3g, Protein 1g

Ingredients:

- Baby carrots – 1/2 pound
- Dried dill – 1/2 tsp.
- Honey – 1/2 tbsp.
- Olive oil – 1/2 tbsp.
- Pepper & salt, to taste

Directions:

Add all ingredients into the bowl and toss well and transfer carrots into the multi-level air fryer basket and place the basket into the instant pot. Seal pot with the air fryer lid. Select air fry mode and cook at 350 F for 12 minutes. Stir halfway through. Serve.

21- Air Fryer Spicy Brussels sprouts

Cook time: 14 minutes | Serves: 2 | Per Serving: Calories 85, Carbs 11g, Fat 4g, Protein 4g

Ingredients:

- Brussels sprouts – 1/2 pound, trimmed and halved
- Chili powder – 1/2 tsp.
- Olive oil – 1/2 tbsp.
- Chives – 1 tbsp., chopped
- Cayenne – 1/2 tsp.
- Pepper & salt, to taste

Directions:

Add all ingredients into the bowl and toss well. Add Brussels sprouts mixture into the multi-level air fryer basket and place the basket into the instant pot. Seal pot with the air fryer lid. Select air fry mode and cook at 370 F for 14 minutes. Stir halfway through. Serve.

22-Cauliflower Broccoli Roast

Cook time: 30 minutes | Serves: 4 | Per Serving: Calories 90, Carbs 6g, Fat 8g, Protein 4g

Ingredients:

- Cauliflower florets – 2 cups
- Broccoli florets – 2 cups
- Olive oil – 2 tbsps.
- Parmesan cheese – 1/4 cup, grated
- Garlic cloves – 3, minced
- Pepper & salt, to taste

Directions:

Add all ingredients into the bowl and mix until well combined. Transfer cauliflower and broccoli mixture into the multi-level air fryer basket and place the basket into the instant pot. Seal pot with the air fryer lid. Select Bake mode and cook at 380 F for 20 minutes. Stir halfway through. Serve.

23-Italian Sweet Potatoes

Cook time: 20 minutes | Serves: 3 | Per Serving: Calories 105, Carbs 8g, Fat 7g, Protein 2g

Ingredients:

- Sweet potato – 1, peeled and cubed
- Butter – 1 tbsp., melted
- Olive oil – 1/2 tbsp.
- Italian seasoning – 1/4 tsp.
- Parmesan cheese – 2 tbsps., grated
- Garlic – 1 tsp., minced

- Garlic salt – 1/4 tsp.

Directions:

Add all ingredients into the mixing bowl and toss well. Transfer sweet potato mixture into the multi-level air fryer basket and place the basket into the instant pot. Seal pot with the air fryer lid. Select Bake mode and cook at 380 F for 20 minutes. Stir halfway through. Serve.

24-Mushroom Beans Roast

Cook time: 20 minutes | Serves: 2 | Per Serving: Calories 87, Carbs 5g, Fat 7g, Protein 2g

Ingredients:

- Green beans – 1 cup, trimmed and cut in half
- Mushrooms – 1 cup, sliced
- Garlic – 1 tsp., minced
- Olive oil – 1 tbsp.
- Onion powder – 1/4 tsp.
- Pepper & salt, to taste

Directions:

Add all ingredients into the bowl and toss well. Transfer green beans & mushroom mixture into the multi-level air fryer basket and place the basket into the instant pot. Seal pot with the air fryer lid. Select Bake mode and cook at 380 F for 20 minutes. Stir halfway through. Serve.

25-Flavorful Broccoli Balls

Cook time: 25 minutes | Serves: 4 | Per Serving: Calories 62, Carbs 7g, Fat 2g, Protein 4g

Ingredients:

- Egg – 1, lightly beaten
- Broccoli florets – 1 cup, steam & chopped
- Cajun seasoning – 1/2 tsp.
- Mozzarella cheese – 1/2 cup, shredded
- Breadcrumbs – 1/4 cup
- Cilantro – 1 tbsp., chopped
- Onion – 2 tbsps., minced
- Pepper & salt, to taste

Directions:

Add all ingredients into the mixing bowl and mix until combined thoroughly. Make small balls and place them into the multi-level air fryer basket and place the basket into the instant pot. Seal pot with the air fryer lid. Select Bake mode and cook at 380 F for 25 minutes. Serve.

26-Crispy Potato Patties

Cook time: 8 minutes | Serves: 4 | Per Serving: Calories 289, Carbs 41g, Fat 8g, Protein 11g

Ingredients:

- Mashed potatoes – 1 cup
- Egg – 1, beaten
- Breadcrumbs – 1 cup
- Flour – 1/2 cup
- Cheddar cheese – 1/2 cup, shredded
- Onion powder – 1/4 tsp.
- Garlic powder – 1/4 tsp.
- Green onion – 2 tbsps., chopped
- Pepper & salt, to taste

Directions:

In a bowl, mix together mashed potatoes, green onion, cheese, onion powder, and garlic powder. Add flour, egg, and breadcrumbs in three separate shallow bowls. Make patties from the potato mixture then roll in flour, dip in eggs, and coat with breadcrumbs. Place patties into the multi-level air fryer basket and place basket into the instant pot. Seal pot with the air fryer lid. Select air fry mode and cook at 370 F for 8 minutes. Serve.

27- Lemon Garlic Mushrooms

Cook time: 10 minutes |Serves: 2 | Per Serving: Calories 90, Carbs 4g, Fat 7g, Protein 4g

Ingredients:

- Mushrooms – 8 oz, cut into quarters
- Olive oil – 1 tbsp.
- Fresh parsley – 1 tbsp., chopped
- Fresh lemon juice – 1 tbsp.
- Soy sauce – 1 tsp.
- Garlic powder – 1/2 tsp.
- Pepper & salt, to taste

Directions:

Add mushrooms in a large bowl and toss with garlic powder, olive oil, soy sauce, pepper, lemon juice and salt. Transfer mushroom mixture into the multi-level air fryer basket and place basket into the instant pot. Seal pot with the air fryer lid. Select air fry mode and cook at 380 F for 10 minutes. Serve.

28- Basil Oregano Potatoes

Cook time: 25 minutes |Serves: 2 | Per Serving: Calories 120, Carbs 27g, Fat 0.2g, Protein 3g

Ingredients:

- Potatoes – 3/4 pound, diced into 1-inch pieces
- Dried oregano – 1/4 tsp.
- Garlic powder – 1/4 tsp.
- Dried basil – 1/4 tsp.
- Pepper & salt, to taste

Directions:

Add potatoes, basil, oregano, garlic powder, pepper, and salt in a mixing bowl and toss well. Transfer potatoes into the multi-level air fryer basket and place basket into the instant pot. Seal pot with the air fryer lid. Select air fry mode and cook at 400 F for 25 minutes. Stir halfway through. Serve.

29-Cheese Mushroom Hasselback Potatoes

Cook time: 40 minutes | Serves: 2 | Per Serving: Calories 285, Carbs 34g, Fat 14g, Protein 7g

Ingredients:

- Potatoes – 2, Using a sharp knife make slits on top
- Butter – 2 tbsps., melted
- Mushrooms – 3 tbsps., sliced
- Parmesan cheese – 4 tbsps., grated
- Pepper & salt, to taste

Directions:

Slide mushroom slices into each slit on the potatoes. Brush Potatoes with melted butter and season with pepper and salt. Place potatoes into the multi-level air fryer basket and place the basket into the instant pot. Seal pot with the air fryer lid. Select air fry mode and cook at 350 F for 20 minutes. Sprinkle parmesan cheese on top of potatoes and air fry for 20 minutes more. Serve.

30-Spicy Potato Fries

Cook time: 20 minutes | Serves: 2 | Per Serving: Calories 188, Carbs 36g, Fat 3g, Protein 4g

Ingredients:

- Potatoes – 1 pound, wash, peel and cut into the shape of fries
- Chili powder – 1/4 tsp.
- Olive oil – 1/2 tbsp.
- Paprika – 1/4 tsp.
- Pepper & salt, to taste

Directions:

Add potato fries in a mixing bowl and drizzle with oil and season with paprika, chili powder, and salt. Transfer potato fries to the multi-level air fryer basket and place the basket into the instant pot. Seal pot with the air fryer lid. Select air fry mode and cook at 370 F for 20 minutes. Stir halfway through. Serve.

POULTRY RECIPES

1-Flavorful Chicken Drumsticks

Cook time: 25 minutes |Serves: 4 | Per Serving: Calories 256, Carbs 3g, Fat 18g, Protein 20g

Ingredients:

- Chicken drumsticks – 1 ½ pound
- Olive oil – 2 tbsps.
- Fresh lime juice – 4 tbsps.
- Cayenne pepper – ½ tsp.
- Black peppercorns – ½ tsp.
- Coriander seeds – ½ tsp.
- Turmeric powder – 1 tsp.
- Dried parsley – 1 tsp.
- Dried oregano– 1 tsp.
- Cumin seeds– 1 tsp.
- Salt – 1 tsp.

Directions:

In a grinder, combine cayenne pepper, peppercorns, coriander seeds, turmeric, parsley, oregano, cumin, and salt and process until finely ground. In a small bowl, mix together ground spices with oil and lime juice. Add chicken drumsticks in a zip-lock bag. Pour spice mixture over chicken drumsticks. Seal zip-lock bag and shake well and place it in the refrigerator overnight. Add marinated chicken drumsticks into the multi-level air fryer basket and place the basket in the instant pot. Seal pot with the air fryer lid, select air fry mode and cook at 400 F for 20-25 minutes. Turn chicken drumsticks halfway through. Serve.

2-Crispy Crust Chicken Breasts

Cook time: 30 minutes |Serves: 2 | Per Serving: Calories 575, Carbs 10g, Fat 35g, Protein 53g

Ingredients:

- Chicken breasts – 2
- Butter – ¼ cup, melted
- Black pepper – 1/8 tsp.
- Cracker crumbs – ½ cup
- Garlic salt – ¼ tsp.

Directions:

Add cracker crumbs and melted butter in two separate shallow dishes. Add black pepper and garlic salt into the cracker crumbs and mix well. Dip chicken breast in melted butter then coat with cracker crumb mixture. Place coated chicken breasts into the multi-level air fryer basket and place basket in the instant pot. Seal pot with the air fryer lid. Select bake mode and cook at 375 F for 25-30 minutes. Turn chicken breasts halfway through. Serve.

3-Baked Chicken Breast

Cook time: 30 minutes | Serves: 2 | Per Serving: Calories 372, Carbs 0.9g, Fat 21.1g, Protein 42.4g

Ingredients:

- Chicken breasts – 2, skinless and boneless
- Garlic powder – 1/4 tsp.
- Onion powder – ¼ tsp.
- Parsley flakes – ½ tsp.
- Paprika – ½ tsp.
- Olive oil – 1 ½ tbsps.
- Black pepper – 1/8 tsp.
- Salt – 1/8 tsp.

Directions:

Add chicken in a large mixing bowl. Add remaining ingredients over chicken breasts and coat well and place them in the refrigerator overnight. Add marinated chicken into the multi-level air fryer basket and place the basket into the instant pot. Seal pot with the air fryer lid. Select bake mode and cook at 375 F for 30 minutes. Turn chicken halfway through. Serve.

4-Simple & Healthy Baked Chicken

Cook time: 25 minutes | Serves: 2 | Per Serving: Calories 342, Carbs 0.3g, Fat 18.2g, Protein 42.3g

Ingredients:

- Chicken breasts – 2, skinless & boneless
- Paprika – 1/8 tsp.
- Seasoning salt – ¼ tsp.
- Italian seasoning – ½ tsp.
- Olive oil – 1 tbsp.
- Black pepper – 1/8 tsp.

Directions:

In a small bowl, mix together oil, Italian seasoning, black pepper, paprika, and seasoning salt and rub all over chicken breasts. Place chicken breasts into the multi-level air fryer basket and place the basket into the instant pot. Seal pot with the air fryer lid. Select bake mode and cook at 380 F for 25 minutes. Serve.

5-Baked Breaded Chicken

Cook time: 30 minutes | Serves: 2 | Per Serving: Calories 513, Carbs 21.4g, Fat 26.3g, Protein 46.2g

Ingredients:

- Chicken breasts – 2, skinless & boneless
- Olive oil – 2 tbsps.
- Garlic cloves – 4, minced
- Breadcrumbs – ½ cup
- Black pepper – ¼ tsp.
- Salt – ¼ tsp.

Directions:

In a shallow bowl, mix together breadcrumbs, black pepper, and salt. In a small bowl, mix together garlic and olive oil and rub over chicken breasts. Coat chicken breasts with breadcrumbs and place them into the multi-level air fryer basket and place basket into the instant pot. Seal pot with air fryer lid. Select bake mode and cook at 380 F for 25-30 minutes. Serve.

6-Dijon Lime Chicken

Cook time: 35 minutes | Serves: 2 | Per Serving: Calories 181, Carbs 2.2g, Fat 7g, Protein 26g

Ingredients:

- Chicken drumsticks – 4
- Dried parsley – ½ tsp.
- Black pepper – ¼ tsp.
- Lime juice – ½
- Garlic clove – 1, minced
- Mayonnaise – ½ tbsp.
- Dijon mustard – 1 ½ tbsps.
- Salt, to taste

Directions:

Add chicken drumsticks into the large mixing bowl. Add remaining ingredients over chicken and toss until well coated. Add chicken drumsticks into the multi-level air fryer basket and place basket into the instant pot. Seal pot with air fryer lid. Select bake mode and cook at 380 F for 35 minutes. Serve.

7-Lemon Pepper Chicken

Cook time: 30 minutes | Serves: 2 | Per Serving: Calories 175, Carbs 4g, Fat 6g, Protein 24g

Ingredients:

- Chicken breasts – 2, skinless & boneless
- Dried oregano – 1 tsp.
- Dried basil – 1 tsp.
- Lemon pepper – 1 ½ tsps.
- Olive oil – 1 tbsp.
- Fresh lemon juice – 2 tbsps.
- Salt – 1/2 tsp.

Directions:

In a small bowl, mix together olive oil, lemon pepper, dried basil, oregano, lemon juice, and salt and rub all over the chicken and let it sit for 10 minutes. Add chicken breasts into the multi-level air fryer basket and place the basket into the instant pot. Seal pot with the air fryer lid. Select bake mode and cook at 350 F for 30 minutes. Serve.

8-Baked Chicken Leg

Cook time: 30 minutes | Serves: 4 | Per Serving: Calories 301, Carbs 2g, Fat 23g, Protein 21g

Ingredients:

- Chicken legs – 4
- Garlic powder – ¼ tsp.
- Paprika – ½ tsp.
- Olive oil – 1 tbsp.
- Black pepper – ¼ tsp.
- Kosher salt – ¼ tsp.

Directions:

In a large mixing bowl, add chicken legs. Pour remaining ingredients over chicken legs and coat well. Place chicken legs into the multi-level air fryer basket and place basket into the instant pot. Seal pot with air fryer lid. Select bake mode and cook at 375 F for 25-30 minutes. Serve.

9-Coconut Chicken

Cook time: 30 minutes | Serves: 3 | Per Serving: Calories 324, Carbs 10.8g, Fat 19.6g, Protein 26.6g

Ingredients:

- Chicken breasts – 3/4 pound, skinless, boneless, & cut into strips
- Shredded unsweetened coconut – ½ cup
- Breadcrumbs – ¼ cup
- Unsweetened coconut milk – ½ cup
- Pepper & salt, to taste

Directions:

Marinate chicken pieces in the coconut milk for overnight. In a shallow bowl, mix together breadcrumbs, shredded coconut, pepper, and salt. Coat marinated chicken pieces with breadcrumb mixture from both the sides. Place coated chicken pieces into the multi-level air fryer basket and place basket in the instant pot. Seal pot with the air fryer lid. Select bake mode and cook at 375 F for 30 minutes. Turn chicken halfway through. Serve.

10-Ranch Baked Chicken

Cook time: 30 minutes | Serves: 3 | Per Serving: Calories 512, Carbs 6g, Fat 29.7g, Protein 52.9g

Ingredients:

- Chicken breasts – 3, boneless & skinless
- Butter – 3 tbsps., melted
- Dry ranch dressing mix – 1 tbsp.
- Parmesan cheese – ½ cup
- Crushed corn flakes – ¾ cup

Directions:

In a shallow bowl, mix together crushed corn flakes, ranch dressing mix, and parmesan cheese. Dip chicken in melted butter and coat with corn flakes mixture.

Place coated chicken into the multi-level air fryer basket and place the basket in the instant pot. Seal pot with the air fryer lid. Select bake mode and cook at 350 F for 30 minutes. Serve.

11-Meatballs

Cook time: 30 minutes | Serves: 4 | Per Serving: Calories 497, Carbs 10.3g, Fat 26.2g, Protein 48.1g

Ingredients:
- Ground chicken– 1 pound
- Onion powder – ½ tsp.
- Garlic powder – ½ tsp.
- Olive oil – 2 tbsps.
- Parmesan cheese – ½ cup, grated
- Breadcrumbs – ½ cup
- Egg – 1, lightly beaten
- Pepper & salt, to taste

Directions:
Add all ingredients into the mixing bowl and mix until well combined. Make small balls and place them into the multi-level air fryer basket and place the basket in the instant pot. Seal pot with the air fryer lid. Select bake mode and cook at 380 F for 25-30 minutes. Serve.

12-Flavorful Chicken Meatballs

Cook time: 30 minutes | Serves: 4 | Per Serving: Calories 367, Carbs 17.1g, Fat 12.9g, Protein 41.5g

Ingredients:
- Ground chicken– 1 pound
- Milk – 2 tbsps.
- Worcestershire sauce – 2 tbsps.
- Egg – 1, lightly beaten
- Red pepper flakes – ¼ tsp.
- Dried basil – 2 tsps.
- Garlic cloves – 2, minced
- Parmesan cheese – ½ cup, grated
- Breadcrumbs– ¾ cup
- Salt – 1 tsp.

Directions:
Add all ingredients into the large bowl and mix until combined thoroughly. Make small balls and place them into the multi-level air fryer basket and place the basket in the instant pot. Seal pot with the air fryer lid. Select bake mode and cook at 380 F for 25-30 minutes. Serve.

13-Crispy Chicken Wings

Cook time: 25 minutes | Serves: 2 | Per Serving: Calories 659, Carbs 4g, Fat 46g, Protein 53g

Ingredients:

- Chicken wings – 12
- Baking powder – 1/2 tbsp.
- Granulated garlic – 1 tsp.
- Chili powder – 1 tbsp.
- Kosher salt – ½ tsp.

Directions:

Add chicken wings into the mixing bowl. Add chili powder, granulated garlic, baking powder, and salt over chicken wings and toss well. Add chicken wings into the multi-level air fryer basket and place the basket in the instant pot. Seal pot with the air fryer lid. Select air fry mode and cook at 400 F for 25 minutes. Turn chicken wings halfway through. Serve.

14-Delicious Parmesan Chicken

Cook time: 15 minutes | Serves: 4 | Per Serving: Calories 269, Carbs 10.6g, Fat 8.9g, Protein 34.4g

Ingredients:

- Chicken breasts – 1 pound, skinless & boneless
- Eggs – 2, lightly beaten
- Herb breadcrumbs – ½ cup
- Parmesan cheese – ½ cup, grated

Directions:

Mix breadcrumbs and parmesan cheese in a shallow dish. In a separate shallow bowl, add eggs. Dip chicken breasts in egg mixture then coat with breadcrumb mixture. Spray multi-level air fryer basket with cooking spray. Place coated chicken breasts into the air fryer basket and place the basket into the instant pot. Seal pot with the air fryer lid. Select air fry mode and cook at 360 F for 15 minutes or until the internal temperature of chicken reaches to 165 F. Serve.

15-Flavorful Air Fryer Chicken

Cook time: 14 minutes | Serves: 4 | Per Serving: Calories 255, Carbs 8.3g, Fat 13.2g, Protein 24.5g

Ingredients:

- Chicken breasts – 1 pound, boneless
- Cayenne pepper – ¼ tsp.
- Italian seasoning – 1 tsp.
- Coconut aminos – 1 tbsp.
- Dijon mustard – 1 tbsp.
- Mayonnaise – ½ cup.
- Black pepper – ½ tsp.
- Sea salt – 1 tsp.

Directions:

In a small bowl, mix together Dijon mustard, cayenne pepper, Italian seasoning, coconut aminos, mayonnaise, pepper, and salt. Add chicken breasts into the large zip-lock bag. Add marinade over chicken. Seal bag and shake well and place in the refrigerator for overnight. Add marinated chicken breasts into the multi-level air fryer basket. Seal pot with the air fryer lid. Select air fry mode and cook at 400 F for 14 minutes. Turn chicken breasts halfway through. Serve.

16-Perfect Chicken Thighs

Cook time: 15 minutes | Serves: 4 | Per Serving: Calories 130, Carbs 2g, Fat 4g, Protein 20g

Ingredients:

- Chicken thighs – 4, skinless & bone-in
- Ground ginger – ¼ tsp.
- Paprika – 2 tsps.
- Garlic powder – 2 tsps.
- Black pepper – ¼ tsp.
- Salt – 1 tsp.

Directions:

In a small bowl, mix together ground ginger, paprika, garlic powder, black pepper, and salt and rub over chicken thighs. Place chicken thighs into the multi-level air fryer basket and place the basket into the instant pot. Seal pot with the air fryer lid. Select air fry mode and cook at 400 F for 15 minutes. Turn chicken thighs after 10 minutes. Serve.

17-Cheesy Chicken Fritters

Cook time: 10 minutes | Serves: 4 | Per Serving: Calories 304, Carbs 12.7g, Fat 13.6g, Protein 36g

Ingredients:

- Ground chicken – 1 pound
- Breadcrumbs – ½ cup
- Green onion – 2 tbsps., chopped
- Pepper – 1 tsp.
- Onion powder – 1 tsp.
- Garlic powder – 1 tsp.
- Provolone cheese – ¼ cup, shredded
- Parmesan cheese – ¼ cup, shredded
- Salt– 1 tsp.

Directions:

In a mixing bowl, mix together all ingredients until combined thoroughly. Place the dehydrating tray in a multi-level air fryer basket. Make patties from the mixture and place on a dehydrating tray. Place the air fryer basket into the instant pot. Seal pot with the air fryer lid. Select air fry mode and cook at 350 F for 10 minutes. Serve.

18-Tasty Chicken Thighs

Cook time: 20 minutes | Serves: 4 | Per Serving: Calories 140, Carbs 1g, Fat 4g, Protein 21g

Ingredients:

- Chicken thighs – 4, skinless & boneless
- Brown sugar – 1 tsp.
- Cumin – ½ tsp.
- Oregano – ½ tsp.
- Paprika – ½ tsp.
- Black pepper – ¼ tsp.
- Salt – ½ tsp.

Directions:

In a small bowl, mix together brown sugar, black pepper, cumin, oregano, paprika, and salt and rub all over chicken thighs. Place chicken thighs into the air fryer basket and place the basket into the instant pot. Seal pot with the air fryer lid. Select air fry mode and cook at 350 F for 20 minutes. Turn chicken halfway through. Serve.

19-Juicy & Delicious Chicken Breast

Cook time: 20 minutes │Serves: 2 │ Per Serving: Calories 385, Carbs 16.7g, Fat 13g, Protein 46.5g

Ingredients:

- Chicken breasts – 2, skinless & boneless
- Egg – 1, lightly beaten
- Parsley – ½ tsp.
- Granulated garlic – ½ tsp.
- Cornflakes cereal – 1 cup
- Salt – ½ tsp.

Directions:

Add cornflake cereal, parsley, garlic, and salt into the food processor and process until nicely crushed. Add cornflakes mixture into the shallow bowl. Add egg in a separate shallow bowl. Dip chicken in egg mixture then coat with cornflake mixture. Place coated chicken in the multi-level air fryer basket and place the basket into the instant pot. Seal pot with the air fryer lid. Select air fry mode and cook at 375 F for 20 minutes. Turn chicken halfway through. Serve.

20-Hot Chicken Wings

Cook time: 30 minutes │Serves: 4 │ Per Serving: Calories 428, Carbs 0.5g, Fat 24.2g, Protein 49.5g

Ingredients:

- Chicken wings – 1 ½ pounds
- Hot sauce – ½ cup
- Butter – ¼ cup, melted
- Pepper & salt, to taste

Directions:

Season chicken wings with pepper and salt. Add chicken wings into the multi-level air fryer basket and place the basket into the instant pot. Seal pot with the air fryer lid. Select air fry mode and cook at 375 F for 20 minutes. Turn chicken wings halfway through. Turn temperature to 400 F and air fry wings for 10 minutes more.

In a mixing bowl, mix together melted butter and hot sauce. Add chicken wings into the sauce and toss until well coated. Serve.

21-Delicious Chicken Tenders

Cook time: 8 minutes |Serves: 4 | Per Serving: Calories 330, Carbs 5.5g, Fat 16.8g, Protein 39.5g

Ingredients:

- Chicken tenders – 1 pound
- Egg – 1, lightly beaten
- Almond flour – ½ cup
- Nutritional yeast – 2 tbsps.
- Black pepper – ½ tsp.
- Salt – ½ tsp.

Directions:

Add egg in a shallow bowl. In a separate, shallow bowl, mix together almond flour and nutritional yeast. Season chicken tenders with pepper and salt. Dip chicken tenders in egg and coat with the almond flour mixture. Place coated chicken tenders in a multi-level air fryer basket and place the basket into the instant pot. Seal pot with the air fryer lid. Select air fry mode and cook at 400 F for 8 minutes. Serve.

22-Parmesan Chicken Nuggets

Cook time: 30 minutes |Serves: 4 | Per Serving: Calories 335, Carbs 4.4g, Fat 14.6g, Protein 43.8g

Ingredients:

- Chicken breasts – 1 ½ pounds, cut into chunks
- Garlic powder – ½ tsp.
- Parmesan cheese – 6 tbsps., shredded
- Mayonnaise – ¼ cup
- Salt – ½ tsp.

Directions:

Line the multi-level air fryer basket with parchment paper and set aside. In a medium bowl, mix together mayonnaise, shredded cheese, garlic powder, and salt. Coat chicken chunks with the mayo mixture and place into the air fryer basket and place the basket into the instant pot. Seal pot with the air fryer lid. Select bake mode and cook at 380 F for 25-30 minutes. Serve.

23-Easy Lemon Pepper Chicken Breast

Cook time: 30 minutes |Serves: 4 | Per Serving: Calories 284, Carbs 1.6g, Fat 10.9g, Protein 42.5g

Ingredients:

- Chicken breasts – 4, boneless & skinless
- Granulated garlic – ½ tsp.
- Lemon pepper seasoning – 1 tbsp.
- Salt – 1 tsp.

Directions:

Season chicken breasts with garlic, lemon pepper seasoning, and salt. Place chicken into the multi-level air fryer basket and place the basket into the instant pot. Seal pot with the air fryer lid. Select air fry mode and cook at 360 F for 30 minutes. Turn chicken halfway through. Serve.

24-Honey Chicken Drumsticks
Cook time: 15 minutes |Serves: 2 | Per Serving: Calories 140, Carbs 6g, Fat 7.3g, Protein 12.7g
Ingredients:
- Chicken drumsticks – 2
- Olive oil – 2 tsp.
- Honey – 2 tsp.
- Garlic – ½ tsp., minced

Directions:
Add chicken drumsticks, oil, honey, and garlic into the zip-lock bag. Seal bag and shake well and place in the refrigerator for 30 minutes. Place marinated chicken drumsticks into the multi-level air fryer basket and place the basket into the instant pot. Seal pot with the air fryer lid. Select air fry mode and cook at 400 F for 15 minutes. Serve.

25-Healthy Chicken Wings
Cook time: 16 minutes |Serves: 3 | Per Serving: Calories 141, Carbs 23.4g, Fat 4g, Protein 4.2g
Ingredients:
- Chicken wings – 9
- Garlic salt – ½ tbsp.
- Brown sugar – 6 tbsps.
- Black pepper – ¼ tbsp.
- Garlic powder – 1 tbsp.
- Chili powder – ½ tbsp.
- Paprika – ½ tbsp.

Directions:
Add chicken wings into the large bowl. Add remaining ingredients over chicken and toss until well coated. Add chicken wings into the multi-level air fryer basket and place the basket into the instant pot. Seal pot with the air fryer lid. Select air fry mode and cook at 400 F for 16 minutes. Turn chicken wings halfway through. Serve.

26-Sriracha Chicken Wings
Cook time: 34 minutes |Serves: 4 | Per Serving: Calories 361, Carbs 19.3g, Fat 16.3g, Protein 33.3g
Ingredients:
- Chicken wings – 1 pound
- Fresh lime juice – 2 tbsps.
- Butter – 1 tbsp.
- Soy sauce – 1 ½ tbsps.

- Sriracha sauce – 2 tbsps.
- Honey – ¼ cup.

Directions:

Add chicken wings into the multi-level air fryer basket and place the basket into the instant pot. Seal pot with the air fryer lid. Select air fryer mode and cook at 360 F for 30 minutes. Turn chicken wings halfway through. While wings are cooking add honey, sriracha sauce, soy sauce, butter, and lime juice in a pan and cook for 4 minutes. Add wings into the mixing bowl. Pour sauce over wings and toss until coated thoroughly. Serve.

27-Flavorful Tandoori Chicken

Cook time: 16 minutes | Serves: 2 | Per Serving: Calories 231, Carbs 4.3g, Fat 12.7g, Protein 22.6g

Ingredients:

- Chicken drumsticks – 4
- For marinade:
- Fresh lime juice – 1 tbsp.
- Ground cumin – 1 tsp.
- Garam masala – ½ tsp.
- Turmeric powder – ½ tsp.
- Chili powder – 1 tsp.
- Ginger garlic powder– 2 tbsps.
- Yogurt– ¼ cup
- Salt – 1 tsp.

Directions:

In a mixing bowl, mix together all marinade ingredients. Add chicken drumsticks into the marinade and coat thoroughly and place in the refrigerator for 1 hour. Add marinated chicken drumsticks into the multi-level air fryer basket and place the basket into the instant pot. Seal pot with the air fryer lid. Select air fry mode and cook at 360 F for 16 minutes. Turn chicken drumsticks halfway through. Serve.

28-Sweet & Spicy Chicken Wings

Cook time: 30 minutes | Serves: 3 | Per Serving: Calories 143, Carbs 25.7g, Fat 3.7g, Protein 3.5g

Ingredients:

- Chicken wings – 12
- Honey – ¼ cup.
- Hot sauce – ½ cup.
- Pepper & salt, to taste

Directions:

Season chicken wings with pepper and salt. Add chicken wings into the multi-level air fryer basket and place basket into the instant pot. Seal pot with air fryer lid. Select air fry mode and cook at 400 F for 25 minutes. While chicken wings are cooking, add honey and hot sauce into the small saucepan and cook for 5 minutes.

Add cooked chicken wings into the large bowl. Pour sauce over chicken wings and toss well. Serve.

29-Vinegar Lemon Chicken Breasts

Cook time: 20 minutes | Serves: 4 | Per Serving: Calories 544, Carbs 3.2g, Fat 38.3g, Protein 42.8g

Ingredients:

- Chicken breasts – 4
- For marinade:
- Lemon juice – 2 tbsps.
- Garlic salt – 2 tsps.
- Olive oil – ½ cup
- Black pepper – 2 tsps.
- Poultry seasoning – 3 tsps.
- Vinegar – 1 cup
- Salt – 1 ½ tbsps.

Directions:

Add all marinade ingredients into the zip-lock bag and mix well. Add chicken into the marinade. Seal bag and place in the refrigerator for overnight. Remove chicken from marinade and place into the multi-level air fryer basket and place the basket into the instant pot. Seal pot with the air fryer lid. Select air fry mode and cook at 350 F for 20 minutes. Turn chicken halfway through. Serve.

30-BBQ Chicken Drumsticks

Cook time: 25 minutes | Serves: 4 | Per Serving: Calories 181, Carbs 11.8g, Fat 9g, Protein 12.8g

Ingredients:

- Chicken drumsticks – 4
- Olive oil – 2 tbsps.
- Onion powder – ¼ tsp.
- Paprika – ¼ tsp.
- Garlic powder – ½ tsp.
- BBQ sauce – 6 tbsps.
- Black pepper – 1/8 tsp.
- Salt – ¼ tsp.

Directions:

In a small bowl, mix together oil, onion powder, paprika, garlic powder, pepper, and salt and rub all over chicken drumsticks. Add chicken drumsticks into the multi-level air fryer basket and place the basket into the instant pot. Seal pot with the air fryer lid. Select air fry mode and cook at 400 F for 15 minutes. Turn chicken drumsticks and air fry for 5 minutes. Baste chicken drumsticks with BBQ sauce and air fry for 5 minutes more. Serve.

31-Soy Honey Chicken

Cook time: 16 minutes | Serves: 4 | Per Serving: Calories 465, Carbs 15g, Fat 27g, Protein 43g

Ingredients:

- Chicken thighs – 1 ½ pounds
- For marinade:
- Ground ginger – ¼ tsp.
- Garlic powder – ½ tsp.
- Honey – 3 tbsps.
- Olive oil – ¼ cup
- Soy sauce – 1/3 cup
- Pepper & salt, to taste

Directions:

Add all marinade ingredients into the large mixing bowl and mix well. Add chicken and coat well. Cover bowl and place in the refrigerator overnight. Remove marinated chicken from marinade and place into the multi-level air fryer basket and place the basket into the instant pot. Seal pot with the air fryer lid. Select air fry mode and cook at 400 F for 16 minutes. Turn chicken halfway through. Serve.

32-Simple Garlic Butter Chicken

Cook time: 16 minutes | Serves: 4 | Per Serving: Calories 329, Carbs 0.2g, Fat 16.6g, Protein 42.3g

Ingredients:

- Chicken breasts – 4, boneless
- Garlic powder – ¼ tsp.
- Butter – 2 tbsps., melted
- Black pepper – ¼ tsp.
- Salt – ½ tsp.

Directions:

In a small bowl, mix together butter, garlic powder, black pepper, and salt and rub over chicken breasts. Place chicken breasts into the multi-level air fryer basket and place the basket into the instant pot. Seal pot with the air fryer lid. Select air fry mode and cook at 380 F for 16 minutes. Turn chicken halfway through. Serve.

33-Juicy Chicken Breast

Cook time: 10 minutes | Serves: 4 | Per Serving: Calories 281, Carbs 1.1g, Fat 15.5g, Protein 33g

Ingredients:

- Chicken tenderloins – 1 pound
- Greek seasoning – 1 tbsp.
- Olive oil – 2 tbsps.

Directions:

Add chicken, Greek seasoning and olive oil into the large mixing bowl and coat well. Place chicken into the multi-level air fryer basket and place the basket into the instant pot. Seal pot with the air fryer lid. Select air fry mode and cook at 380 F for 10 minutes. Serve.

34-Delicious Turkey Burger Patties

Cook time: 12 minutes | Serves: 4 | Per Serving: Calories 230, Carbs 2.1g, Fat 12.5g, Protein 31.3g

Ingredients:

- Ground turkey – 1 pound
- Garlic – 1 tsp., minced
- Small onion – 1, diced
- Jalapeno pepper – 1, diced
- Pepper & salt, to taste

Directions:

Add all ingredients into the mixing bowl and mix until thoroughly combined. Make four equal shaped patties and place them into the multi-level air fryer basket and place the basket into the instant pot. Seal pot with the air fryer lid. Select air fry mode and cook at 380 F for 12 minutes. Turn patties halfway through. Serve.

35-Parmesan Chicken Wings

Cook time: 30 minutes | Serves: 4 | Per Serving: Calories 329, Carbs 2g, Fat 19.3g, Protein 35.4g

Ingredients:

- Chicken wings – 1 pound
- Parmesan cheese – ¼ cup, grated
- Butter – 3 tbsps., melted
- Herb & garlic seasoning – ½ tsp.

Directions:

Add chicken wings into the multi-level air fryer basket and place the basket into the instant pot. Seal pot with the air fryer lid. Select air fry mode and cook at 380 F for 30 minutes. Turn chicken wings halfway through. In a mixing bowl, mix together melted butter, cheese, and seasoning. Add cooked chicken wings in a bowl and toss to coat. Serve.

36-Asian Chicken Wings

Cook time: 25 minutes | Serves: 4 | Per Serving: Calories 305, Carbs 21g, Fat 8.4g, Protein 35g

Ingredients:

- Chicken wings – 1 pound
- Garlic powder – 1 tbsp.
- Brown sugar – ½ cup
- Soy sauce – ½ cup

Directions:

In a small saucepan, add garlic powder, brown sugar, and soy sauce and bring to boil. Stir constantly because it will burn quickly. In a large bowl, add chicken wings. Pour sauce over chicken wings and coat well. Cover bowl and place in the refrigerator for

30 minutes. Add marinated chicken wings into a multi-level air fryer basket and place the basket into the instant pot. Seal pot with the air fryer lid. Select air fry mode and cook at 360 F for 25 minutes. Turn chicken wings after 10 minutes. Serve.

37-Tasty Sesame Chicken

Cook time: 30 minutes | Serves: 2 | Per Serving: Calories 435, Carbs 8.1g, Fat 25g, Protein 43.9g

Ingredients:
- Chicken breasts – 2, boneless
- Onion powder – 1 tbsp.
- Garlic powder – 1 tbsp.
- Paprika – 1 tbsp.
- Sesame oil – 2 tbsps.
- Black pepper – ½ tsp.
- Kosher salt – 1 tsp.

Directions:
In a small bowl, mix together onion powder, garlic powder, paprika, oil, pepper, and salt and rub all over chicken breasts. Place chicken breasts into the multi-level air fryer basket and place the basket into the instant pot. Seal pot with the air fryer lid. Select air fry mode and cook at 380 F for 30 minutes. Turn chicken after 20 minutes. Serve.

38-Flavorful Tandoori Chicken Thighs

Cook time: 30 minutes | Serves: 4 | Per Serving: Calories 295, Carbs 10.8g, Fat 9.9g, Protein 37.4g

Ingredients:
- Chicken thighs – 1 pound
- For marinade:
- Ground turmeric – ½ tsp.
- Chili powder – 1 tsp.
- Ground cumin – 2 tsps.
- Vinegar – ¼ cup
- Ginger garlic paste – 2 tbsps.
- Yogurt – 1 cup
- Salt – ½ tsp.

Directions:
Add all marinade ingredients into the large mixing bowl and mix well. Add chicken and coat thoroughly. Cover bowl and place in the refrigerator for 1 hour. Remove chicken from marinade and place in a multi-level air fryer basket and place the basket into the instant pot. Seal pot with the air fryer lid. Select air fry mode and cook at 350 F for 30 minutes. Turn chicken halfway through. Serve.

39-Spicy Hasselback Chicken

Cook time: 16 minutes | Serves: 2 | Per Serving: Calories 530, Carbs 2g, Fat 30g, Protein 41g

Ingredients:
- Chicken breasts – 2, skinless & boneless
- Cheddar cheese – ½ cup, shredded
- Pickled jalapenos – ¼ cup, chopped
- Cream cheese – 2 oz
- Bacon slices – 4, cooked and crumbled

Directions:
In a bowl, mix together ¼ cup cheddar cheese, cream cheese, jalapenos, and bacon and set aside. Using a sharp knife make six slits on top of chicken breasts. Stuff cheese mixture into the slits. Place chicken into the multi-level air fryer basket and place basket into the instant pot. Seal pot with the air fryer lid. Select air fry mode and cook at 350 F for 15 minutes. Top with remaining cheese and air fry for 1 minute. Serve.

40-Southern Chicken Thighs
Cook time: 20 minutes |Serves: 4 | Per Serving: Calories 289, Carbs 2.3g, Fat 10.8g, Protein 42.2g

Ingredients:
- Chicken thighs – 4
- Southern seasoning – 1 1/2 tbsps.

Directions:
Rub chicken thighs with southern seasoning. Place chicken thighs into the multi-level air fryer basket and place the basket into the instant pot. Seal pot with the air fryer lid. Select air fry mode and cook at 360 F for 20 minutes. Turn chicken halfway through. Serve.

41-Air Fryer Turkey Breast
Cook time: 40 minutes |Serves: 3 | Per Serving: Calories 228, Carbs 7g, Fat 10.2g, Protein 26g

Ingredients:
- Turkey breast – 1 pound
- Fresh rosemary – 1 tsp., chopped
- Fresh thyme – 1 tsp., chopped
- Garlic clove – 1, minced
- Butter – 4 tbsps., melted
- Pepper & salt, to taste

Directions:
In a small bowl, mix together melted butter, garlic, thyme, rosemary, pepper, and salt and brush all over turkey breast. Place turkey breast into the multi-level air fryer basket and place the basket into the instant pot. Seal pot with the air fryer lid. Select air fry mode and cook at 375 F for 40 minutes. Slice and serve.

42-Juicy Turkey Patties
Cook time: 16 minutes |Serves: 4 | Per Serving: Calories 179, Carbs 11g, Fat 3g, Protein 28g

Ingredients:

- Ground turkey – 1 pound
- Breadcrumbs – ¼ cup
- Garlic – 1 tsp., minced
- Worcestershire sauce – 2 tsps.
- Ranch seasoning – 1 tbsp.
- Onion – ½, minced
- Apple sauce – ¼ cup
- Pepper & salt, to taste

Directions:

Add all ingredients into the mixing bowl and mix until combined thoroughly. Make patties and place them in the refrigerator for 30 minutes. Remove turkey patties from the refrigerator and place them into the multi-level air fryer basket. Place the basket into the instant pot. Seal pot with the air fryer lid. Select air fry mode and cook at 360 F for 16 minutes. Turn patties halfway through. Serve.

43-Mushroom Turkey Patties

Cook time: 10 minutes │Serves: 4 │ Per Serving: Calories 346, Carbs 10g, Fat 21g, Protein 31g

Ingredients:

- Ground turkey – 1 pound
- Breadcrumbs – 4 tbsps.
- Mustard – 1 tsp.
- Worcestershire sauce – 1 tbsp.
- Fresh parsley – 1 tbsp., chopped
- Garlic cloves – 2, minced
- Small onion – 1, minced
- Mushrooms – 4, chopped
- Pepper & salt, to taste

Directions:

Add all ingredients into the mixing bowl and mix until combined thoroughly. Make patties and place them in the refrigerator for 30 minutes. Remove turkey patties from the refrigerator and place it into the multi-level air fryer basket. Place the basket into the instant pot. Seal pot with the air fryer lid. Select air fry mode and cook at 330 F for 10 minutes. Serve.

44-Turkey Meatballs

Cook time: 10 minutes │Serves: 4 │ Per Serving: Calories 175, Carbs 6g, Fat 3g, Protein 29g

Ingredients:

- Ground turkey – 1 pound
- Soy sauce – 1 tbsp.
- Fresh parsley – 4 tbsps., chopped
- Egg – 1, lightly beaten

- Breadcrumbs – ½ cup
- Pepper & salt, to taste

Directions:

Add all ingredients into the large bowl and mix until combined thoroughly. Make small balls and place them into the multi-level air fryer basket and place basket into the instant pot. Seal pot with the air fryer lid. Select air fry mode and cook at 400 F for 10 minutes. Turn meatballs halfway through. Serve.

45-Spinach Turkey Patties

Cook time: 30 minutes |Serves: 4 | Per Serving: Calories 341, Carbs 8.2g, Fat 17.9g, Protein 40.7g

Ingredients:

- Ground turkey – 1 pound
- Breadcrumbs – 4 tbsps.
- Mozzarella cheese – 4 oz, shredded
- Dried basil – 2 tsps.
- Dried parsley – 2 tsps.
- Worcestershire sauce – 2 tsps.
- Lemon zest – 1 tsp.
- Vinegar – 2 tbsps.
- Small onion– 1/2, minced
- Spinach– 3 cups
- Olive oil – 2 tbsps.
- Pepper & salt, to taste

Directions:

Heat 1 tablespoon of olive oil in a pan over medium heat. Add spinach and sauté until spinach is wilted. Transfer sautéed spinach into the mixing bowl. Add remaining ingredients into the bowl and mix until combined thoroughly. Make patties and place them into the multi-level air fryer basket and place basket into the instant pot. Seal pot with the air fryer lid. Select bake mode and cook at 375 F for 30 minutes. Serve.

PORK RECIPES

1-Parmesan Pork Chops

Cook time: 12 minutes |Serves: 6 | Per Serving: Calories 400, Carbs 1g, Fat 30g, Protein 27g

Ingredients:

- Pork chops – 1 1/2 pounds, boneless
- Almond flour – 1/3 cup
- Paprika – 1 tsp.
- Creole seasoning – 1/2 tsp.
- Garlic powder – 1 tsp.
- Parmesan cheese – 1/4 cup, grated

Directions:

Add all ingredients except pork chops into the zip-lock bag. Add pork chops. Seal bag and shake well. Place pork chops into the multi-level air fryer basket and place basket into the instant pot. Seal pot with the air fryer lid. Select air fry mode and cook at 400 F for 12 minutes. Serve.

2-Flavorful Crispy Crust Pork Chops

Cook time: 17 minutes |Serves: 2 | Per Serving: Calories 365, Carbs 1g, Fat 29g, Protein 23g

Ingredients:

- Pork chops – 2, bone-in
- Onion powder – 1/2 tsp.
- Paprika – 1/2 tsp.
- Parsley – 1/2 tsp.
- Olive oil – 1 tbsp.
- Pork rinds – 1 cup, crushed
- Garlic powder – 1/2 tsp.

Directions:

In a bowl, mix together pork rinds, garlic powder, onion powder, paprika, and parsley. Brush pork chops with oil and coat with pork rind mixture. Place coated pork chops into the multi-level air fryer basket and place the basket into the instant pot. Seal pot with the air fryer lid. Select air fry mode and cook at 400 F for 12 minutes. Turn pork chops and air fry for 5 minutes more. Serve.

3-Easy Ranch Pork Chops

Cook time: 35 minutes |Serves: 4 | Per Serving: Calories 387, Carbs 0g, Fat 33g, Protein 18g

Ingredients:

- Pork chops – 4, boneless
- Olive oil – 4 tbsp.
- Ranch seasoning – 1 1/2 tbsps.

Directions:

Mix together ranch seasoning and olive oil and rub over pork chops. Place pork chops into the multi-level air fryer basket and place basket into the instant pot. Seal pot with the air fryer lid. Select Bake mode and cook at 380 F for 35 minutes. Turn pork chops halfway through. Serve.

4-Breaded Pork Chops

Cook time: 35 minutes | Serves: 4 | Per Serving: Calories 200, Carbs 3g, Fat 15g, Protein 12g

Ingredients:

- Pork chops – 2, boneless
- Paprika – 1/8 tsp.
- Breadcrumbs – 2 tbsps.
- Parmesan cheese – 1/3 cup, grated
- Olive oil – 1 tbsp.
- Garlic powder – 1/4 tsp.
- Dried parsley – 1/2 tsp.
- Pepper & salt, to taste

Directions:

Brush pork chops with olive oil. In a shallow bowl, mix together breadcrumbs, cheese, paprika, parsley, garlic powder, pepper, and salt. Coat pork chops with breadcrumb mixture and place into the multi-level air fryer basket and place the basket into the instant pot. Seal pot with the air fryer lid. Select Bake mode and cook at 350 F for 35 minutes. Turn pork chops halfway through. Serve.

5-Buttery Pork Chops

Cook time: 15 minutes | Serves: 2 | Per Serving: Calories 468, Carbs 2g, Fat 43g, Protein 18g

Ingredients:

- Pork chops – 2
- Butter –4 tbsps., melted
- Garlic cloves – 2, minced
- Thyme – 1 tbsp., chopped
- Pepper & salt, to taste

Directions:

Season pork chops with pepper and salt. Mix together butter, thyme, and garlic and brush over pork chops. Place pork chops into the multi-level air fryer basket and place the basket into the instant pot. Seal pot with the air fryer lid. Select Bake mode and cook at 375 F for 15 minutes. Serve.

6-Moist & Juicy Pork Chops

Cook time: 18 minutes | Serves: 2 | Per Serving: Calories 330, Carbs 3g, Fat 27g, Protein 18g

Ingredients:

- Pork chops – 2, boneless
- Garlic powder – 1 tsp.

- Onion powder – 1 tsp.
- Paprika – 1/2 tbsp
- Olive oil – 1 tbsp.
- Oregano – 1/2 tbsp.
- Pepper & salt, to taste

Directions:

Brush pork chops with oil. Mix together oregano, garlic powder, onion powder, paprika, pepper, and salt and rub all over pork chops. Place pork chops into the multi-level air fryer basket and place the basket into the instant pot. Seal pot with the air fryer lid. Select Bake mode and cook at 380 F for 18 minutes. Turn pork chops halfway through. Serve.

7-Tender Pork Chops

Cook time: 15 minutes Serves: 4 Per Serving: Calories 368, Carbs 1g, Fat 32g, Protein 18g

Ingredients:

- Pork chops – 4, boneless
- Olive oil – 4 tbsps.
- Onion powder – 1 tsp.
- Paprika – 1 tsp.
- Pepper & salt, to taste

Directions:

Brush pork chops with oil. Mix together onion powder, paprika, pepper, and salt and rub over pork chops. Place pork chops into the multi-level air fryer basket and place the basket into the instant pot. Seal pot with air fryer lid. Select Bake mode and cook at 380 F for 15 minutes. Turn pork chops halfway through. Serve.

8-Parmesan Crisp Pork Chops

Cook time: 30 minutes Serves: 3 Per Serving: Calories 358, Carbs 7g, Fat 25g, Protein 23g

Ingredients:

- Pork chops – 3, boneless
- Milk – 2 tbsps.
- Egg –1, lightly beaten
- Parmesan cheese – 3 tbsps., grated
- Crackers – 1/2 cup, crushed
- Pepper & salt, to taste

Directions:

In a shallow bowl, whisk egg and milk. In a separate shallow bowl, mix together cheese, crushed crackers, pepper, and salt. Dip pork chops in egg then coat with cheese mixture and place into the multi-level air fryer basket and place the basket into the instant pot. Seal pot with the air fryer lid. Select Bake mode and cook at 350 F for 30 minutes. Turn pork chops halfway through. Serve.

9-Sriracha Pork Chops

Cook time: 30 minutes | Serves: 4 | Per Serving: Calories 360, Carbs 18g, Fat 23g, Protein 19g

Ingredients:

- Pork chops – 4
- Garlic – 1 tbsp., minced
- Honey – 3 tbsps.
- Soy sauce – 1/3 cup
- Sesame oil – 1 tbsp.
- Lime juice – 1
- Sriracha – 2 tbsps.
- Ground ginger – 1 tsp.

Directions:

Add pork chops into the zip-lock bag. Pour remaining ingredients over pork chops. Seal bag and place in the refrigerator for 1 hour. Remove pork chops from marinade and place them into the multi-level air fryer basket and place the basket into the instant pot. Seal pot with the air fryer lid. Select Bake mode and cook at 375 F for 30 minutes. Turn pork chops halfway through. Serve.

10-Garlic Mustard Pork Chops

Cook time: 30 minutes | Serves: 4 | Per Serving: Calories 479, Carbs 24g, Fat 28g, Protein 28g

Ingredients:

- Pork chops – 1 pound
- Brown mustard – 2 tbsps.
- Garlic salt – 1 tsp.
- Flour – 1 cup

Directions:

Mix together flour and garlic salt. Coat one side of pork chops with flour and place into the air fryer basket. Spread mustard on one side of pork chops. Place air fryer basket into the instant pot. Seal pot with the air fryer lid. Select bake mode and cook at 350 F for 30 minutes. Turn pork chops halfway through. Serve.

11-Meatballs

Cook time: 20 minutes | Serves: 4 | Per Serving: Calories 241, Carbs 12g, Fat 5g, Protein 33g

Ingredients:

- Ground pork – 1 pound
- Egg – 1, lightly beaten
- Breadcrumbs – 1/2 cup
- Garlic – 1 tbsp., minced
- Small onion – 1, chopped
- Pepper & salt, to taste

Directions:

Add all ingredients into the mixing bowl and mix until well combined. Make small balls from the meat mixture and place them into the multi-level air fryer basket and place the basket into the instant pot. Seal pot with the air fryer lid. Select Bake mode and cook at 380 F for 20 minutes. Serve.

12-Cheesy Meatballs

Cook time: 20 minutes | Serves: 4 | Per Serving: Calories 215, Carbs 5g, Fat 6g, Protein 33g

Ingredients:
- Ground pork – 1 pound
- Egg – 1, lightly beaten
- Garlic cloves – 2, minced
- Onion – 1/2, chopped
- Dried parsley – 1/2 tbsp.
- Ketchup – 3 tbsps.
- Parmesan cheese – 4 tbsps., grated
- Pepper & salt, to taste

Directions:
Add all ingredients into the bowl and mix until well combined. Make small balls from the meat mixture and place them into the multi-level air fryer basket and place the basket into the instant pot. Seal pot with the air fryer lid. Select Bake mode and cook at 380 F for 20 minutes. Serve.

13-Meatloaf

Cook time: 20 minutes | Serves: 4 | Per Serving: Calories 211, Carbs 6g, Fat 5g, Protein 32g

Ingredients:
- Ground pork – 1 pound
- Egg – 1, lightly beaten
- Breadcrumbs – 3 tbsps.
- Onion – 1, chopped
- Thyme – 1 tbsp., chopped
- Pepper & salt, to taste

Directions:
Spray a loaf pan with cooking spray and set aside. Add all ingredients into the bowl and mix until well combined. Pour meat mixture into the loaf pan. Place steam rack into the instant pot. Place loaf pan on top of the steam rack. Seal pot with the air fryer lid. Select bake mode and cook at 380 F for 20 minutes. Serve.

14-Maple Mustard Pork Chops

Cook time: 12 minutes | Serves: 3 | Per Serving: Calories 330, Carbs 9g, Fat 23g, Protein 21g

Ingredients:
- Pork chops – 3
- Maple syrup – 1 tbsp.

- Mustard – 3 tbsps.
- Garlic – 1 tbsp., minced
- Pepper & salt, to taste

Directions:

In a small bowl, mix together mustard, garlic, maple syrup, pepper, and salt. Brush pork chops with the mustard mixture and place into the multi-level air fryer basket and place the basket into the instant pot. Seal pot with the air fryer lid. Select air fry mode and cook at 350 F for 12 minutes. Turn pork chops halfway through. Serve.

15-Meatballs

Cook time: 15 minutes │Serves: 4 │ Per Serving: Calories 117, Carbs 6g, Fat 7g, Protein 6g

Ingredients:

- Pork sausage – 4 oz
- Breadcrumbs – 3 tbsps.
- Onion – 1, chopped
- Sage – 1 tsp.
- Garlic – 1/2 tsp., minced
- Pepper & salt, to taste

Directions:

Add all ingredients into the bowl and mix until combined thoroughly. Make small balls from the meat mixture and place it into the multi-level air fryer basket and place the basket into the instant pot. Seal pot with the air fryer lid. Select air fry mode and cook at 340 F for 15 minutes. Serve.

16-Cheese Mustard Meatballs

Cook time: 10 minutes │Serves: 4 │ Per Serving: Calories 197, Carbs 3g, Fat 5g, Protein 31g

Ingredients:

- Ground pork – 1 pound
- Maple syrup – 1/2 tsp.
- Onion – 1, chopped
- Cheddar cheese – 2 tbsps., grated
- Mustard – 2 tsps.
- Pepper & salt, to taste

Directions:

Add all ingredients into the bowl and mix until combined thoroughly. Make small balls from the meat mixture and place it into the multi-level air fryer basket and place the basket into the instant pot. Seal pot with the air fryer lid. Select air fry mode and cook at 400 F for 10 minutes. Serve.

17-Pork with Veggies

Cook time: 20 minutes │Serves: 3 │ Per Serving: Calories 174, Carbs 12g, Fat 7g, Protein 16g

Ingredients:

- Pork tenderloin – 6 oz, cut into strips
- Bell peppers – 3, cut into strips
- Onion – 1, chopped
- Olive oil – 1 tbsp.
- Pepper & salt, to taste

Directions:

Add all ingredients into the large bowl and toss well. Transfer the meat mixture into the multi-level air fryer basket and place the basket into the instant pot. Seal pot with the air fryer lid. Select air fry mode and cook at 390 F for 20 minutes. Stir halfway through. Serve.

18-Herb Pork Chops

Cook time: 16 minutes | Serves: 2 | Per Serving: Calories 322, Carbs 1g, Fat 27g, Protein 18g

Ingredients:

- Pork chops – 2
- Rosemary – 1 tbsp., chopped
- Olive oil – 1 tbsp.
- Thyme – 1/4 tbsp., chopped
- Pepper & salt, to taste

Directions:

Mix together oil, rosemary, thyme, pepper, and salt and rub all over pork chops. Place pork chops into the multi-level air fryer basket and place the basket into the instant pot. Seal pot with the air fryer lid. Select air fry mode and cook at 400 F for 16 minutes. Turn pork chops halfway through. Serve.

19-Tarragon Mustard Pork

Cook time: 25 minutes | Serves: 4 | Per Serving: Calories 287, Carbs 2g, Fat 15g, Protein 34g

Ingredients:

- Pork stew meat – 1 pound, cubed
- Lime juice – 1/2
- Tarragon – 1/2 tsp., chopped
- Olive oil – 1 tbsp.
- Mustard – 1 tbsp.
- Chives – 1 tbsp., chopped
- Garlic clove – 1, minced
- Pepper & salt, to taste

Directions:

Add all ingredients into the mixing bowl and toss well. Transfer meat mixture into the multi-level air fryer basket and place the basket into the instant pot. Seal pot with the air fryer lid. Select air fry mode and cook at 380 F for 25 minutes. Stir halfway through. Serve.

20-Crispy Pork Chunks

Cook time: 12 minutes | Serves: 4 | Per Serving: Calories 478, Carbs 29g, Fat 10g, Protein 62g

Ingredients:

- Eggs – 2, lightly beaten
- Pork – 2 pounds, cut into chunks
- Cornstarch – 1 cup
- Pepper & salt, to taste

Directions:

In a bowl, mix together cornstarch, pepper, and salt. In a shallow bowl, add beaten eggs. Coat meat chunks with cornstarch and dip each chunk into the egg mixture then coat with cornstarch. Place coated meat chunks into the multi-level air fryer basket and place the basket into the instant pot. Seal pot with the air fryer lid. Select air fry mode and cook at 340 F for 12 minutes. Serve.

21-Basil Cheese Meatballs

Cook time: 15 minutes | Serves: 2 | Per Serving: Calories 130, Carbs 4g, Fat 3g, Protein 19g

Ingredients:

- Pork – 5 oz, minced
- Cheddar cheese – 1/2 tbsp., grated
- Fresh basil – 1/2 tbsp.
- Onion –1/2, diced
- Mustard – 1/2 tsp.
- Honey – 1/2 tsp.
- Garlic paste – 1/2 tsp.
- Pepper & salt, to taste

Directions:

Add all ingredients into the bowl and mix until thoroughly combined. Make small balls from the meat mixture and place it into the multi-level air fryer basket and place the basket into the instant pot. Seal pot with the air fryer lid. Select air fry mode and cook at 390 F for 15 minutes. Serve.

22-Honey & Ginger Pork Chops

Cook time: 10 minutes | Serves: 2 | Per Serving: Calories 295, Carbs 9g, Fat 19g, Protein 18g

Ingredients:

- Pork loin chops – 2
- Balsamic vinegar – 1/2 tsp.
- Ground ginger – 1/8 tsp.
- Soy sauce – 1 tbsp.
- Garlic clove – 1, minced
- Honey – 1 tbsp.
- Pepper & salt, to taste

Directions:

Season pork chops with pepper. In a bowl, mix together honey, soy sauce, garlic, ground ginger, and vinegar. Add seasoned pork chops in a bowl and coat well. Cover and place in the refrigerator for 1 hour. Remove pork chops from marinade and place them into the multi-level air fryer basket and place the basket into the instant pot. Seal pot with the air fryer lid. Select air fry mode and cook at 350 F for 10 minutes. Serve.

23-Flavorful BBQ Pork Chops

Cook time: 15 minutes |Serves: 2 | Per Serving: Calories 289, Carbs 6g, Fat 20g, Protein 18g

Ingredients:

- Pork chops – 2
- For rub:
- Garlic powder – 1 tsp.
- Chili powder – 1/2 tsp.
- Paprika – 1/2 tsp.
- Allspice – 1/2 tsp.
- Dry mustard – 1/2 tsp.
- Ground cumin – 1 tsp.
- Brown sugar – 1 tbsp.
- Salt

Directions:

In a small bowl, mix together all rub ingredients and rub all over pork chops. Place pork chops into the multi-level air fryer basket and place the basket into the instant pot. Seal pot with the air fryer lid. Select air fry mode and cook at 400 F for 15 minutes. Serve.

24-Cheese Herb Pork Chops

Cook time: 15 minutes |Serves: 4 | Per Serving: Calories 410, Carbs 20g, Fat 24g, Protein 26g

Ingredients:

- Pork chops – 4
- Eggs – 2, lightly beaten
- Sugar – 1 tsp.
- Parmesan cheese – 1/3 cup, grated
- Breadcrumbs – 1/3 cup
- Flour – 1/2 cup
- Thyme – 1/2 tsp.
- Oregano – 1/2 tsp.
- Basil – 1/2 tsp.
- Garlic powder – 1/2 tsp.
- Pepper & salt, to taste

Directions:

Season pork chops with pepper and salt. In a shallow bowl, mix together breadcrumbs, cheese, sugar, garlic powder, basil, oregano, and thyme. Dredge pork chops in flour then dip in egg and coat with breadcrumbs mixture. Place coated pork chops into the multi-level air fryer basket and place the basket into the instant pot. Seal pot with the air fryer lid. Select air fry mode and cook at 360 F for 15 minutes. Turn pork chops halfway through. Serve.

25-Rosemary Lemon Pork Chops

Cook time: 16 minutes |Serves: 2 | Per Serving: Calories 337, Carbs 5g, Fat 27g, Protein 18g

Ingredients:

- Pork chops – 2
- Red pepper flakes – 1/2 tsp.
- Fennel seeds – 1 tsp., crushed
- Sage – 1 tsp., chopped
- Olive oil – 1 tbsp.
- Lemon zest – 1, grated
- Garlic – 1 tsp., minced
- Rosemary – 2 tsps., chopped
- Pepper & salt, to taste

Directions:

Mix together oil, lemon zest, garlic, red pepper flakes, fennel seeds, sage, rosemary, pepper, and salt and rub all over pork chops. Place pork chops into the multi-level air fryer basket and place the basket into the instant pot. Seal pot with the air fryer lid. Select air fry mode and cook at 380 F for 16 minutes. Turn pork chops halfway through. Serve.

26-Moist Pork Chops

Cook time: 12 minutes |Serves: 4 | Per Serving: Calories 270, Carbs 0.8g, Fat 21g, Protein 18g

Ingredients:

- Pork chops – 4
- Paprika – 1 tsp.
- Olive oil – 1 tsp.
- Onion powder – 1 tsp.
- Pepper & salt, to taste

Directions:

Brush pork chops with oil and season with paprika, onion powder, pepper, and salt. Place pork chops into the multi-level air fryer basket and place the basket into the instant pot. Seal pot with the air fryer lid. Select air fry mode and cook at 380 F for 12 minutes. Turn pork chops halfway through. Serve.

27-Garlicky Pork Bites

Cook time: 15 minutes |Serves: 4 | Per Serving: Calories 525, Carbs 0.5g, Fat 30g, Protein 52g

Ingredients:

- Pork belly – 1 pound, cut into 3/4-inch cubes
- Garlic powder – 1/2 tsp.
- Soy sauce – 1 tsp.
- Pepper & salt, to taste

Directions:

In a mixing bowl, toss pork cubes, garlic powder, soy sauce, pepper, and salt. Add pork cubes into the multi-level air fryer basket and place the basket into the instant pot. Seal pot with the air fryer lid. Select air fry mode and cook at 400 F for 15 minutes. Turn halfway through. Serve.

28-Sweet & Spicy Pork Chops

Cook time: 15 minutes | Serves: 4 | Per Serving: Calories 362, Carbs 19g, Fat 23g, Protein 18g

Ingredients:

- Pork chops – 4
- Garlic cloves – 2, minced
- Honey – 1/4 cup
- Olive oil – 1 tbsp.
- Sweet chili sauce – 1 tbsp.
- Fresh lemon juice – 2 tbsps.
- Pepper & salt, to taste

Directions:

Season pork chops with pepper and salt. Place pork chops into the multi-level air fryer basket and place the basket into the instant pot. Seal pot with the air fryer lid. Select air fry mode and cook at 400 F for 15 minutes. Meanwhile, in a pan heat oil over medium heat. Add garlic and sauté for 30 seconds. Add lemon juice, sweet chili sauce, and honey and cook until sauce thickens. Brush pork chops with honey garlic sauce. Serve.

29-Dijon Pork Chops

Cook time: 14 minutes | Serves: 4 | Per Serving: Calories 347, Carbs 14g, Fat 23g, Protein 18g

Ingredients:

- Pork chops – 4, boneless
- Maple syrup – 4 tbsps.
- Montreal seasoning – 1 tbsp.
- Fresh lemon juice – 2 tsps.
- Dijon mustard – 2 tbsps.
- Olive oil – 1 tbsp.
- Salt

Directions:

Brush pork chops with oil and rub with Montreal seasoning and salt. Place pork chops into the multi-level air fryer basket and place the basket into the instant pot.

Seal pot with the air fryer lid. Select air fry mode and cook at 375 F for 14 minutes. Turn halfway through. Place cooked pork chops on a plate. Mix together lemon juice, mustard, and maple syrup and pour over pork chops. Serve.

30-Simple Paprika Pork Chops
Cook time: 10 minutes | Serves: 3 | Per Serving: Calories 262, Carbs 0.6g, Fat 20g, Protein 18g
Ingredients:
- Pork chops – 3
- Garlic powder – 1/4 tsp.
- Olive oil – 2 tsps.
- Paprika – 1/2 tsp.
- Pepper & salt, to taste

Directions:
Brush pork chops with oil and season with garlic powder, paprika, pepper, and salt. Place pork chops into the multi-level air fryer basket and place the basket into the instant pot. Seal pot with the air fryer lid. Select air fry mode and cook at 380 F for 10 minutes. Turn halfway through. Serve.

31-Meatballs
Cook time: 20 minutes | Serves: 4 | Per Serving: Calories 263, Carbs 11g, Fat 8g, Protein 37g
Ingredients:
- Ground pork – 8 oz
- Ground beef – 8 oz
- Egg – 1, lightly beaten
- Parsley – 4 tbsps., chopped
- Garlic – 1 tsp., minced
- Onion – 1/2, chopped
- Parmesan cheese – 4 tbsps., grated
- Breadcrumbs – 1/2 cup
- Pepper & salt, to taste

Directions:
Add all ingredients into the large bowl and mix until combined thoroughly. Make small balls from the meat mixture and place it into the multi-level air fryer basket and place the basket into the instant pot. Seal pot with the air fryer lid. Select air fry mode and cook at 380 F for 20 minutes. Turn halfway through. Serve.

32-Italian Pork Chops
Cook time: 35 minutes | Serves: 4 | Per Serving: Calories 314, Carbs 2g, Fat 24g, Protein 20g
Ingredients:
- Pork chops – 4, boneless and thick-cut
- Feta cheese – 1/2 cup, crumbled
- Garlic cloves – 2, minced

- Fresh parsley – 2 tbsps., chopped
- Olives – 2 tbsps., chopped
- Sun-dried tomatoes – 2 tbsps., chopped

Directions:

In a bowl, mix together feta cheese, garlic, parsley, olives, and sun-dried tomatoes. Stuff cheese mixture into the pork chops and season with pepper and salt. Place pork chops into the multi-level air fryer basket and place the basket into the instant pot. Seal pot with the air fryer lid. Select air fry mode and cook at 375 F for 35 minutes. Serve.

33-Rosemary Pork Chops

Cook time: 15 minutes | Serves: 4 | Per Serving: Calories 262, Carbs 1g, Fat 20g, Protein 18g

Ingredients:

- Pork chops – 4, boneless
- Dried rosemary – 1 tsp., crushed
- Fresh rosemary – 1 tbsp., chopped
- Garlic cloves – 2, minced
- Pepper & salt, to taste

Directions:

Season pork chops with pepper and salt. Mix together dried rosemary, garlic, and rosemary and rub over pork chops. Place pork chops into the multi-level air fryer basket and place the basket into the instant pot. Seal pot with the air fryer lid. Select air fry mode and cook at 380 F for 15 minutes. Turn pork chops halfway through. Serve.

34-Flavorful Pork Chops

Cook time: 12 minutes | Serves: 4 | Per Serving: Calories 441, Carbs 3g, Fat 33g, Protein 29g

Ingredients:

- Pork chops – 1 pound, boneless
- Almond flour – 1/3 cup
- Onion powder – 1/4 tsp.
- Chili powder – 1/4 tsp.
- Paprika – 1 tsp.
- Creole seasoning – 1 tsp.
- Garlic powder – 1 tsp.
- Cheddar cheese – 1/4 cup., shredded

Directions:

Add all ingredients except pork chops into the zip-lock bag. Add pork chops into the bag. Seal bag and shake well. Place pork chops into the multi-level air fryer basket and place the basket into the instant pot. Seal pot with the air fryer lid. Select air fry mode and cook at 400 F for 12 minutes. Turn pork chops halfway through. Serve.

35-Meatballs

Cook time: 15 minutes | Serves: 2 | Per Serving: Calories 130, Carbs 4g, Fat 3g, Protein 19g

Ingredients:

- Ground pork – 5 oz
- Fresh basil – 1/2 tbsp.
- Onion – 1/2, diced
- Mustard – 1/2 tsp.
- Honey – 1/2 tsp.
- Garlic paste – 1/2 tsp.
- Cheddar cheese – 1/2 tbsp., grated
- Pepper & salt, to taste

Directions:

Add all ingredients into the mixing bowl and mix until combined thoroughly. Make small balls from the meat mixture and place it into the multi-level air fryer basket and place the basket into the instant pot. Seal pot with the air fryer lid. Select air fry mode and cook at 390 F for 15 minutes. Serve.

BEEF & LAMB RECIPES

1-Garlic Lime Beef
Cook time: 25 minutes | Serves: 4 | Per Serving: Calories 253, Carbs 2g, Fat 10g, Protein 35g

Ingredients:

- Beef stew meat – 1 pound, cut into strips
- Garlic clove – 1, minced
- Lime juice – 1/2
- Olive oil – 1 tbsp.
- Chives – 1/2 tbsp., chopped
- Ground cumin – 1/2 tbsp.
- Garlic powder – 1 tbsp.
- Pepper & salt, to taste

Directions:

Add the meat into the large bowl. Add remaining ingredients over the meat and toss well. Transfer meat into the multi-level air fryer basket and place the basket into the instant pot. Seal pot with the air fryer lid. Select air fry mode and cook at 380 F for 25 minutes. Stir meat halfway through. Serve.

2-Meatballs
Cook time: 20 minutes | Serves: 6 | Per Serving: Calories 188, Carbs 7g, Fat 5g, Protein 24g

Ingredients:

- Ground beef – 8 oz
- Egg – 1, lightly beaten
- Parsley – 1/4 cup, chopped
- Garlic – 1 tsp., minced
- Onion – 1/2, diced
- Ground pork – 8 oz
- Parmesan cheese – 1/4 cup, grated
- Breadcrumbs – 1/2 cup
- Pepper & salt, to taste

Directions:

Add all ingredients into the bowl and mix until combined thoroughly. Make small balls from the meat mixture and place them into the multi-level air fryer basket and place basket into the instant pot. Seal pot with the air fryer lid. Select bake mode and cook at 380 F for 20 minutes. Serve.

3-Cheesy Burger Patties
Cook time: 15 minutes | Serves: 6 | Per Serving: Calories 297, Carbs 1g, Fat 10g, Protein 47g

Ingredients:

- Ground beef – 2 pounds
- Garlic powder – 1 tsp.

- Garlic salt – 2 tsps.
- Mozzarella cheese – 1 cup, grated
- Onion powder – 1 tsp.

Directions:
Add all ingredients into the mixing bowl and mix until combined thoroughly. Make patties from the meat mixture and place into the multi-level air fryer basket and place the basket into the instant pot. Seal pot with the air fryer lid. Select bake mode and cook at 380 F for 15 minutes. Serve.

4-Meatballs
Cook time: 25 minutes | Serves: 4 | Per Serving: Calories 235, Carbs 1g, Fat 9g, Protein 33g
Ingredients:
- Ground lamb – 1 pound
- Egg – 1, lightly beaten
- Oregano – 2 tsps., chopped
- Parsley – 2 tbsps., chopped
- Garlic – 1 tbsp., minced
- Red pepper flakes – 1/4 tsp.
- Ground cumin – 1 tsp.
- Pepper & salt, to taste

Directions:
Add all ingredients into the bowl and mix until combined thoroughly. Make small balls from the meat mixture and place them into the multi-level air fryer basket and place basket into the instant pot. Seal pot with the air fryer lid. Select bake mode and cook at 380 F for 25 minutes. Serve.

5-Basil Parmesan Meatballs
Cook time: 20 minutes | Serves: 4 | Per Serving: Calories 311, Carbs 12g, Fat 10g, Protein 39g
Ingredients:
- Ground beef – 1 pound
- Parsley – 1 tbsp., chopped
- Rosemary – 1 tbsp., chopped
- Milk – 2 tbsps.
- Small onion – 1/2, chopped
- Parmesan cheese – 1/4 cup, grated
- Egg – 1, lightly beaten
- Garlic cloves – 2, minced
- Basil – 1, chopped
- Breadcrumbs – 1/2 cup
- Pepper & salt, to taste

Directions:

Add all ingredients into the bowl and mix until combined thoroughly. Make small balls from the meat mixture and place them into the multi-level air fryer basket and place the basket into the instant pot. Seal pot with the air fryer lid. Select bake mode and cook at 375 F for 20 minutes. Serve.

6-Baked Meatballs
Cook time: 15 minutes | Serves: 4 | Per Serving: Calories 233, Carbs 1g, Fat 8g, Protein 36g
Ingredients:
- Ground beef – 1 pound
- Garlic powder – 1 tsp.
- Onion powder – 1 tsp.
- Parmesan cheese – 1/4 cup, grated
- Pepper & salt, to taste

Directions:
Add all ingredients into the bowl and mix until combined thoroughly. Make small balls from the meat mixture and place them into the multi-level air fryer basket and place the basket into the instant pot. Seal pot with the air fryer lid. Select bake mode and cook at 380 F for 20 minutes. Serve.

7-Beef with Broccoli
Cook time: 25 minutes | Serves: 2 | Per Serving: Calories 304, Carbs 7g, Fat 14g, Protein 35g
Ingredients:
- Beef stew meat – 1/2 pound, cut into pieces
- Broccoli florets – 1/2 cup
- Garlic clove – 1, minced
- Olive oil – 1 tbsp.
- Onion – 1, sliced
- Pepper & salt, to taste

Directions:
Add meat and remaining ingredients into the mixing bowl and toss well. Transfer meat mixture into the multi-level air fryer basket and place the basket into the instant pot. Seal pot with the air fryer lid. Select air fry mode and cook at 390 F for 25 minutes. Stir halfway through. Serve.

8-Garlic Mint Lamb Chops
Cook time: 20 minutes | Serves: 4 | Per Serving: Calories 280, Carbs 2g, Fat 15g, Protein 32g
Ingredients:
- Lamb chops – 1 pound
- Lime juice – 1
- Mint – 2 tbsps., chopped
- Olive oil – 2 tbsps.
- Paprika – 1 tsp.

- Garlic – 1, minced
- Pepper & salt, to taste

Directions:

Add lamb chops into the bowl. Pour remaining ingredients over lamb chops and coat well. Place lamb chops into the multi-level air fryer basket and place the basket into the instant pot. Seal pot with the air fryer lid. Select air fry mode and cook at 400 F for 20 minutes. Serve.

9-Meatballs

Cook time: 12 minutes │Serves: 4 │ Per Serving: Calories 77, Carbs 1g, Fat 5g, Protein 6g

Ingredients:

- Egg – 1, lightly beaten
- Lamb meat – 4 oz, minced
- Oregano – 1 tbsp., chopped
- Lemon zest – 1/2 tbsp.
- Pepper & salt, to taste

Directions:

Add all ingredients into the bowl and mix until well combined. Make small balls from meat mixture and place them into the multi-level air fryer basket and place basket into the instant pot. Seal pot with air fryer lid. Select bake mode and cook at 380 F for 15 minutes. Serve.

10-Beef Patties

Cook time: 16 minutes │Serves: 4 │ Per Serving: Calories 235, Carbs 7g, Fat 7g, Protein 32g

Ingredients:

- Ground beef – 14 oz
- Ham – 1 oz, cut into strips
- Breadcrumbs – 3 tbsps.
- Leek – 1, chopped
- Pepper & salt, to taste

Directions:

Add all ingredients into the bowl and mix until well combined. Make small patties from meat mixture and place it into the multi-level air fryer basket and place basket into the instant pot. Seal pot with air fryer lid. Select air fry mode and cook at 390 F for 16 minutes. Turn patties halfway through. Serve.

11-Meatloaf

Cook time: 25 minutes │Serves: 4 │ Per Serving: Calories 235, Carbs 7g, Fat 7g, Protein 32g

Ingredients:

- Ground beef – 14 oz
- Egg – 1, lightly beaten
- Breadcrumbs – 3 tbsps.

- Onion – 1, chopped
- Mushrooms – 1/2 cup, sliced
- Thyme – 1 tbsp.
- Pepper & salt, to taste

Directions:

Spray a loaf pan with cooking spray and set aside. Add all ingredients into the bowl and mix until well combined. Pour meat mixture into the prepared loaf pan. Place steam rack into the instant pot. Place loaf pan on top of the steam rack. Seal pot with air fryer lid. Select air fry mode and cook at 390 F for 25 minutes. Serve.

12-Delicious Mint Lamb Patties

Cook time: 30 minutes | Serves: 4 | Per Serving: Calories 266, Carbs 12g, Fat 14g, Protein 20g

Ingredients:

- Ground lamb meat – 1 pound
- Egg – 1, lightly beaten
- Cilantro – 1 tbsp. , chopped
- Garlic – 1/2 tbsp. , minced
- Almond meal – 1/4 cup
- Mint – 1 tbsp. , chopped
- Pepper & salt, to taste

Directions:

Add all ingredients into the bowl and mix until well combined. Make small patties from meat mixture and place it into the multi-level air fryer basket and place basket into the instant pot. Seal pot with air fryer lid. Select air fry mode and cook at 390 F for 30 minutes. Turn patties halfway through. Serve.

13-Cilantro Lime Lamb Chops

Cook time: 24 minutes | Serves: 3 | Per Serving: Calories 264, Carbs 1g, Fat 14g, Protein 30g

Ingredients:

- Lamb chops – 6
- Cilantro – 1/4 cup, chopped
- Olive oil – 1 1/2 tbsps.
- Lime juice – 1/2
- Garlic – 1/2 tsp. , minced
- Green chili pepper – 1/2, minced
- Pepper & salt, to taste

Directions:

Add lamb chops in a bowl with remaining ingredients and coat well. Place lamb chops into the multi-level air fryer basket and place basket into the instant pot. Seal pot with air fryer lid. Select air fry mode and cook at 400 F for 24 minutes. Turn lamb chops halfway through. Serve.

14-Lemon Garlic Lamb Chops
Cook time: 24 minutes | Serves: 4 | Per Serving: Calories 138, Carbs 1g, Fat 7g, Protein 15g
Ingredients:
- Lamb chops – 4
- Garlic clove – 1, minced
- Mint – 1/2 cup, chopped
- Olive oil – 1 tbsp.
- Lemon juice – 1/2
- Pepper & salt, to taste

Directions:
Add oil, lemon juice, garlic, mint, pepper, and salt into the food processor and process until smooth. Add lamb chops in a bowl. Pour blended mixture over lamb chops and coat well. Place lamb chops into the multi-level air fryer basket and place basket into the instant pot. Seal pot with air fryer lid. Select air fry mode and cook at 400 F for 24 minutes. Turn lamb chops halfway through. Serve.

15-Lamb with Bell Pepper
Cook time: 20 minutes | Serves: 4 | Per Serving: Calories 305, Carbs 3g, Fat 22g, Protein 21g
Ingredients:
- Lamb meat – 1 pound, cubed
- Bell pepper – 1, cut into chunks
- Dried oregano – 1/2 tbsp.
- Garlic – 1/2 tbsp. , minced
- Olive oil – 2 tbsps.
- Vinegar – 1/2 tbsp.
- Lemon juice – 1 tbsp.
- Dried rosemary – 1/4 tsp.
- Pepper & salt, to taste

Directions:
Add all ingredients into the mixing bowl and toss well. Transfer meat mixture into the multi-level air fryer basket and place basket into the instant pot. Seal pot with air fryer lid. Select air fry mode and cook at 380 F for 20 minutes. Serve.

16-Italian Lamb
Cook time: 30 minutes | Serves: 4 | Per Serving: Calories 336, Carbs 8g, Fat 23g, Protein 22g
Ingredients:
- Lamb meat – 1 pound, cubed
- Garlic – 1 tbsp. , minced
- Olives – 1/4 cup, sliced
- Olive oil – 2 tbsps.
- Rosemary springs – 2, chopped
- Lemon zest – 1, grated

- Pepper & salt, to taste

Directions:

Add all ingredients into the mixing bowl and toss well. Transfer meat mixture into the multi-level air fryer basket and place basket into the instant pot. Seal pot with air fryer lid. Select air fry mode and cook at 380 F for 30 minutes. Stir halfway through. Serve.

17-Cheese Rosemary Lamb Cutlets

Cook time: 30 minutes |Serves: 4 | Per Serving: Calories 194, Carbs 2g, Fat 12g, Protein 17g

Ingredients:

- Lamb cutlets – 4
- Parmesan cheese – 2 tbsps. , grated
- Shredded coconut – 1/4 cup
- Olive oil – 1 1/2 tbsps.
- Rosemary – 1/2 tbsp. , chopped
- Chives – 1 tbsp. , chopped
- Parsley – 1 tbsp. , chopped
- Mustard – 1 1/2 tbsps.
- Pepper & salt, to taste

Directions:

Add cutlets into the large bowl with remaining ingredients except for cheese and shredded coconut and toss well. In a shallow dish, mix together cheese and shredded coconut. Coat lamb cutlets with cheese mixture and place into the multi-level air fryer basket and place basket into the instant pot. Seal pot with air fryer lid. Select air fry mode and cook at 390 F for 30 minutes. Turn lamb cutlets halfway through. Serve.

18-Meatballs

Cook time: 30 minutes |Serves: 4 | Per Serving: Calories 317, Carbs 2g, Fat 18g, Protein 34g

Ingredients:

- Ground lamb – 1 pound
- Egg – 1, lightly beaten
- Thyme – 1 tbsp., chopped
- Pine nuts – 1/4 cup, toasted and chopped
- Olive oil – 1 tbsp.
- Garlic – 1 tsp., minced
- Pepper & salt, to taste

Directions:

Add all ingredients into the bowl and mix until thoroughly combined. Make small balls from the meat mixture and place them into the multi-level air fryer basket and place the basket into the instant pot. Seal pot with the air fryer lid. Select air fry mode and cook at 380 F for 30 minutes. Turn meatballs halfway through. Serve.

19-Greek Lamb Cutlets

Cook time: 30 minutes |Serves: 4 | Per Serving: Calories 171, Carbs 1g, Fat 11g, Protein 15g

Ingredients:

- Lamb cutlets – 4
- Garlic cloves – 3
- Mint leaves – 1/4 cup
- Olive oil – 2 tbsps.
- Lemon juice – 1 1/2 tbsps.
- Coriander seeds – 1/2 tbsp.
- Ground cumin – 1/2 tbsp.
- Pepper & salt, to taste

Directions:

Add garlic, mint, oil, lemon juice, coriander seeds, cumin, pepper, and salt into the blender and blend until smooth. Rub blended mixture over lamb cutlets and place them into the multi-level air fryer basket and place the basket into the instant pot. Seal pot with the air fryer lid. Select air fry mode and cook at 380 F for 30 minutes. Turn lamb cutlets halfway through. Serve.

20-Garlic Rosemary Lamb Cutlets

Cook time: 30 minutes |Serves: 4 | Per Serving: Calories 135, Carbs 1g, Fat 7g, Protein 15g

Ingredients:

- Lamb cutlets – 4
- Olive oil – 1 tbsp.
- Cayenne – 1/8 tsp.
- Garlic clove – 1, minced
- Rosemary – 1 tbsp., chopped
- Pepper & salt, to taste

Directions:

Add lamb cutlets into the bowl with the remaining ingredients and coat well. Arrange cutlets into the multi-level air fryer basket and place the basket into the instant pot. Seal pot with the air fryer lid. Select air fry mode and cook at 380 F for 30 minutes. Turn lamb cutlets halfway through. Serve.

21-Meatballs

Cook time: 12 minutes |Serves: 4 | Per Serving: Calories 75, Carbs 0.3g, Fat 5g, Protein 6g

Ingredients:

- Ground lamb meat – 4 oz
- Egg – 1, lightly beaten
- Oregano – 1 tbsp., chopped
- Lemon zest – 1/2 tbsp.
- Pepper & salt, to taste

Directions:

Add all ingredients into the bowl and mix until thoroughly combined. Make small balls from the meat mixture and place them into the multi-level air fryer basket and place the basket into the instant pot. Seal pot with the air fryer lid. Select air fry mode and cook at 400 F for 12 minutes. Serve.

22-Chili Garlic Lamb Chops
Cook time: 20 minutes | Serves: 4 | Per Serving: Calories 135, Carbs 1g, Fat 7g, Protein 15g
Ingredients:
- lamb chops – 4
- Chili powder – 1/2 tsp.
- Garlic – 1 tbsp., minced
- Olive oil – 1 tbsp.
- Paprika – 1/4 tsp.
- Pepper & salt, to taste

Directions:
Add lamb chops into the bowl with the remaining ingredients and coat well. Arrange lamb chops into the multi-level air fryer basket and place the basket into the instant pot. Seal pot with the air fryer lid. Select air fry mode and cook at 390 F for 20 minutes. Turn lamb chops halfway through. Serve.

23-Meatloaf
Cook time: 35 minutes | Serves: 4 | Per Serving: Calories 243, Carbs 1g, Fat 10g, Protein 33g
Ingredients:
- Ground lamb – 1 pound
- Ground cumin – 1/2 tsp.
- Cilantro – 1 tbsp., chopped
- Parsley – 1 tbsp, chopped
- Olive oil – 1 tsp.
- Paprika – 1/2 tsp.
- Lemon juice – 1/2 tsp.
- Scallions – 2, chopped
- Tomato sauce – 1 tbsp.
- Egg – 1, lightly beaten
- Ground coriander – 1/2 tsp.
- Cinnamon – 1/4 tsp.
- Pepper & salt, to taste

Directions:
Spray a loaf pan with cooking spray and set aside. Add all ingredients into the bowl and mix until thoroughly combined. Pour the meat mixture into the prepared loaf pan. Place steam rack into the instant pot. Place loaf pan on top of the steam rack. Select air fry mode and cook at 380 F for 35 minutes. Serve.

24-Basil Pesto Lamb Chops

Cook time: 20 minutes | Serves: 4 | Per Serving: Calories 250, Carbs 1g, Fat 12g, Protein 32g

Ingredients:

- Lamb chops – 1 pound
- Chives – 1 tbsp, chopped
- Paprika – 1 1/2 tbsps.
- Garlic – 1, minced
- Basil pesto – 2 tsps.
- Olive oil – 1 tbsp.
- Pepper & salt, to taste

Directions:

Add lamb chops into the bowl with the remaining ingredients and coat well. Arrange lamb chops into the multi-level air fryer basket and place the basket into the instant pot. Seal pot with the air fryer lid. Select air fry mode and cook at 380 F for 25 minutes. Turn lamb chops halfway through. Serve.

25-Asian Lamb Steak

Cook time: 15 minutes | Serves: 4 | Per Serving: Calories 227, Carbs 3g, Fat 8g, Protein 32g

Ingredients:

- Lamb chops – 1 pound, boneless
- Cayenne – 1 tsp.
- Cardamom powder – 1/4 tsp.
- Garam masala – 1/2 tsp.
- Garlic cloves – 3
- Ginger –1 tbsp., sliced
- Ground fennel – 1/4 tsp.
- Onion – 1/2, sliced
- Salt

Directions:

Add all ingredients except meat into the blender and blend until smooth. Add the meat into the large bowl. Pour blended mixture over meat and coat well. Cover and marinate meat for 30 minutes. Place marinated meat into the multi-level air fryer basket and place the basket into the instant pot. Seal pot with the air fryer lid. Select air fry mode and cook at 330 F for 15 minutes. Turn meat halfway through. Serve.

26-Meatballs

Cook time: 15 minutes | Serves: 2 | Per Serving: Calories 301, Carbs 1g, Fat 13g, Protein 42g

Ingredients:

- Ground lamb – 1/2 pound
- Garlic cloves – 1, minced
- Coriander – 1/2 tbsp., chopped
- Egg white – 1

- Mint – 1/2 tbsp., chopped
- Turkey – 2 oz
- Olive oil – 1/2 tbsp.
- Parsley – 1 tbsp., chopped
- Salt – 1/2 tsp.

Directions:

Add all ingredients into the bowl and mix until thoroughly combined. Make small balls from the meat mixture and place them into the multi-level air fryer basket and place the basket into the instant pot. Seal pot with the air fryer lid. Select air fry mode and cook at 320 F for 15 minutes. Serve.

27-Burgers Patties

Cook time: 10 minutes | Serves: 2 | Per Serving: Calories 218, Carbs 1g, Fat 7g, Protein 34g

Ingredients:

- Ground beef – 1/2 pound
- Dried parsley – 1/2 tsp.
- Black pepper – 1/4 tsp.
- Onion powder – 1/4 tsp.
- Garlic powder – 1/4 tsp.
- Hot sauce – 1/2 tsp.
- Worcestershire sauce – 1/2 tbsp.
- Salt – 1/4 tsp.

Directions:

Add all ingredients into the bowl and mix until combined thoroughly. Make small patties from the meat mixture and place them into the multi-level air fryer basket and place the basket into the instant pot. Seal pot with the air fryer lid. Select air fry mode and cook at 350 F for 10 minutes. Serve.

28-Delicious Beef Kebab

Cook time: 10 minutes | Serves: 2 | Per Serving: Calories 262, Carbs 4g, Fat 10g, Protein 35g

Ingredients:

- Beef chuck – 1/2 pound, cut into 1-inch pieces
- Sour cream – 2 1/2 tbsps.
- Bell pepper – 1/2, cut into 1-inch pieces
- Onion – 1/4, cut into 1-inch pieces
- Soy sauce – 1 tbsp.

Directions:

In a large bowl, mix together meat, soy sauce, and sour cream. Cover and place in the refrigerator overnight. Thread marinated meat, bell peppers, and onions on soaked wooden skewers. Place skewers into the multi-level air fryer basket and place the basket into the instant pot. Seal pot with the air fryer lid. Select air fry mode and cook at 400 F for 10 minutes. Turn skewers halfway through. Serve.

29-Steak with Potatoes
Cook time: 20 minutes │Serves: 2 │ Per Serving: Calories 318, Carbs 9g, Fat 11g, Protein 42g
Ingredients:
- Steak – 1/2 pound, cut into 1/2-inch cubes
- Potatoes – 1/4 pound, cut into 1/2-inch cubes
- Butter – 1 tbsp., melted
- Garlic powder – 1/4 tsp.
- Worcestershire sauce – 1/2 tsp.
- Pepper & salt, to taste

Directions:
Cook potatoes in boiling water for 5 minutes. Drain well and set aside. In a large bowl, toss together steak cubes, potatoes, garlic powder, Worcestershire sauce, butter, pepper, and salt. Add steak potato mixture into the multi-level air fryer basket and place the basket into the instant pot. Seal pot with the air fryer lid. Select air fry mode and cook at 400 F for 20 minutes. Stir halfway through. Serve.

30-Steak with Mushrooms
Cook time: 20 minutes │Serves: 2 │ Per Serving: Calories 294, Carbs 2g, Fat 11g, Protein 42g
Ingredients:
- Steak – 1/2 pound, cut into 1-inch cubes
- Butter – 1 tbsp., melted
- Mushrooms – 4 oz, sliced
- Garlic powder – 1/4 tsp.
- Worcestershire sauce – 1/2 tbsp.
- Pepper & salt, to taste

Directions:
In a large bowl, toss steak cubes, mushrooms, garlic powder, Worcestershire sauce, butter, pepper, and salt. Add steak mushroom mixture into the multi-level air fryer basket and place the basket into the instant pot. Seal pot with the air fryer lid. Select air fry mode and cook at 400 F for 20 minutes. Stir halfway through. Serve.

FISH & SEAFOOD RECIPES

1-Butter Rosemary Prawns

Cook time: 10 minutes |Serves: 2 | Per Serving: Calories 136, Carbs 2g, Fat 4g, Protein 20g

Ingredients:

- Prawns – 8
- Rosemary – 1 tbsp., chopped
- Butter – 1/2 tbsp., melted
- Pepper & salt, to taste

Directions:

Add prawns, butter, rosemary, pepper, and salt in a mixing bowl and toss well. Cover and place in the refrigerator for 1 hour. Add marinated prawns to the multi-level air fryer basket and place the basket into the instant pot. Seal pot with the air fryer lid. Select air fry mode and cook at 350 F for 10 minutes. Serve.

2-Salmon Patties

Cook time: 8 minutes |Serves: 6 | Per Serving: Calories 192, Carbs 9g, Fat 8g, Protein 18g

Ingredients:

- Can salmon – 14 oz, drained and flakes
- Eggs – 2, lightly beaten
- Lime zest – 1/2
- Brown sugar – 1 tbsp.
- Curry paste – 2 tbsps.
- Breadcrumbs – 1/2 cup
- Salt – 1/4 tsp.

Directions:

Add all ingredients into the mixing bowl and mix well. Make patties from the salmon mixture and place into the multi-level air fryer basket and place the basket into the instant pot. Seal pot with the air fryer lid. Select air fry mode and cook at 360 F for 8 minutes. Turn patties halfway through. Serve.

3-Spicy Shrimp

Cook time: 6 minutes |Serves: 2 | Per Serving: Calories 198, Carbs 2g, Fat 9g, Protein 26g

Ingredients:

- Shrimp – 1/2 pound, peeled and deveined
- Cayenne pepper – 1/2 tsp.
- Olive oil – 1 tbsp.
- Old bay seasoning – 1/2 tsp.
- Paprika – 1/4 tsp.
- Salt – 1/8 tsp.

Directions:

Add all ingredients into the mixing bowl and toss well and spread out in the multi-level air fryer basket and place the basket into the instant pot. Seal pot with the air fryer lid. Select air fry mode and cook at 400 F for 6 minutes. Serve.

4-Crab Patties

Cook time: 10 minutes | Serves: 4 | Per Serving: Calories 90, Carbs 5g, Fat 3g, Protein 7g

Ingredients:
- Crabmeat – 8 oz
- Mayonnaise – 2 tbsps.
- Green onion – 2 tbsps., chopped
- Bell pepper – 1/4 cup, chopped
- Old bay seasoning – 1 tsp.
- Breadcrumbs – 1 tbsp.

Directions:
Add all ingredients into the bowl and mix until well combined. Make patties and place them into the multi-level air fryer basket and place the basket into the instant pot. Seal pot with the air fryer lid. Select air fry mode and cook at 370 F for 10 minutes. Serve.

5-Tuna Patties

Cook time: 20 minutes | Serves: 6 | Per Serving: Calories 91, Carbs 6g, Fat 3g, Protein 8g

Ingredients:
- Tuna – 5 oz, drained
- Egg – 1, lightly beaten
- Mayonnaise – 3 tbsps.
- Celery – 1/4 cup, chopped
- Breadcrumbs – 1/3 cup

Directions:
Add all ingredients into the bowl and mix until thoroughly combined. Make patties from the tuna mixture and place into the multi-level air fryer basket and place the basket into the instant pot. Seal pot with the air fryer lid. Select bake mode and cook at 380 F for 20 minutes. Turn patties halfway through. Serve.

6-Delicious Crab Cakes

Cook time: 15 minutes | Serves: 4 | Per Serving: Calories 145, Carbs 17g, Fat 2g, Protein 10g

Ingredients:
- Crabmeat – 1/2 pound, flakes
- Dry mustard – 1/8 tsp.
- Red pepper flakes – 1/8 tsp.
- Breadcrumbs – 3/4 cup
- Paprika – 1/4 tsp.
- Worcestershire sauce – 1/2 tsp.

- Mayonnaise – 1/2 tbsp.
- Lemon juice – 1/2 tbsp.
- Yogurt – 1 tbsp.
- Parsley – 1 tbsp., chopped
- Green onions – 1/4 cup, chopped

Directions:

Add all ingredients into the bowl and mix until thoroughly combined. Make patties from the crab mixture and place into the multi-level air fryer basket and place the basket into the instant pot. Seal pot with the air fryer lid. Select bake mode and cook at 350 F for 15 minutes. Turn patties halfway through. Serve.

7-Crab Balls

Cook time: 20 minutes │Serves: 4 │ Per Serving: Calories 154, Carbs 6g, Fat 9g, Protein 10g

Ingredients:

- Crabmeat – 4 oz
- Egg – 1, lightly beaten
- Cream cheese – 2 tbsps.
- Mozzarella cheese – 1/2 cup, shredded
- Jalapeno pepper – 1/4 cup, chopped
- Paprika – 1/4 tbsp.
- Breadcrumbs – 1/4 cup
- Cheddar cheese – 1/2 cup, shredded
- Pepper & salt, to taste

Directions:

Add all ingredients into the bowl and mix until thoroughly combined. Make small balls from the crab mixture and place them into the multi-level air fryer basket and place the basket into the instant pot. Seal pot with the air fryer lid. Select bake mode and cook at 375 F for 20 minutes. Serve.

8-Salmon Cakes

Cook time: 20 minutes │Serves: 4 │ Per Serving: Calories 244, Carbs 13g, Fat 9g, Protein 25g

Ingredients:

- Salmon – 12 oz, drain and flaked with a fork
- Eggs – 2, lightly beaten
- Parsley – 2 tbsps., chopped
- Celery – 1/2 cup, diced
- Bell pepper – 1/2 cup, diced
- Breadcrumbs – 1/2 cup
- Dijon mustard – 1 tbsp.
- Garlic powder – 1 tsp.
- Onion – 1/2, diced
- Pepper & salt, to taste

Directions:

Add all ingredients into the bowl and mix until thoroughly combined. Make small patties from the salmon mixture and place them into the multi-level air fryer basket and place the basket into the instant pot. Seal pot with the air fryer lid. Select bake mode and cook at 380 F for 20 minutes. Turn patties halfway through. Serve.

9-Lemon Pepper Shrimp

Cook time: 8 minutes |Serves: 2 | Per Serving: Calories 251, Carbs 6g, Fat 6g, Protein 39g

Ingredients:

- Shrimp – 12, peeled and deveined
- Paprika – 1/4 tsp.
- Lemon pepper – 1 tsp.
- Lemon juice – 1
- Olive oil – 1/2 tbsp.
- Lemon – 1, sliced
- Garlic powder – 1/4 tsp.

Directions:

Add all ingredients into the bowl and toss well. Transfer shrimp mixture into a multi-level air fryer basket and place the basket into the instant pot. Seal pot with the air fryer lid. Select air fry mode and cook at 400 F for 8 minutes. Serve.

10-Easy Shrimp Fajitas

Cook time: 12 minutes |Serves: 6 | Per Serving: Calories 55, Carbs 2g, Fat 1g, Protein 9g

Ingredients:

- Shrimp – 1/2 pound
- Onion – 1/4 cup, diced
- Bell pepper – 1, diced
- Taco seasoning – 1 tbsp.
- Pepper & salt, to taste

Directions:

Add all ingredients into the bowl and toss well. Transfer shrimp mixture into a multi-level air fryer basket and place the basket into the instant pot. Seal pot with the air fryer lid. Select air fry mode and cook at 390 F for 12 minutes. Serve.

11-Old Bay Seasoned Shrimp

Cook time: 6 minutes |Serves: 2 | Per Serving: Calories 195, Carbs 2g, Fat 9g, Protein 25g

Ingredients:

- Shrimp – 1/2 pound, peeled and deveined
- Old bay seasoning – 1/2 tsp.
- Cayenne – 1/2 tsp.
- Olive oil – 1 tbsp.
- Paprika – 1/4 tsp.

- Salt

Directions:

Add all ingredients into the bowl and toss well. Transfer shrimp mixture into the multi-level air fryer basket and place the basket into the instant pot. Seal pot with the air fryer lid. Select air fry mode and cook at 390 F for 6 minutes. Serve.

12-Easy Cajun Shrimp

Cook time: 10 minutes | Serves: 4 | Per Serving: Calories 195, Carbs 1g, Fat 9g, Protein 25g

Ingredients:

- Shrimp – 1 pound, deveined & peeled
- Olive oil – 2 tbsps.
- Cajun seasoning – 1/2 tbsp.

Directions:

Add shrimp, Cajun seasoning, and oil into the mixing bowl and toss well. Add shrimp into the multi-level air fryer basket and place the basket into the instant pot. Seal pot with the air fryer lid. Select bake mode and cook at 350 F for 10 minutes. Serve.

13-Lemon Pepper White Fish Fillets

Cook time: 10 minutes | Serves: 2 | Per Serving: Calories 358, Carbs 1g, Fat 19g, Protein 41g

Ingredients:

- White fish fillets – 12 oz
- Onion powder – 1/2 tsp.
- Lemon pepper seasoning – 1/2 tsp.
- Garlic powder – 1/2 tsp.
- Olive oil – 1 tbsp.
- Pepper & salt, to taste

Directions:

Brush fish fillets with olive oil and season with onion powder, lemon pepper seasoning, garlic powder, pepper, and salt. Place fish fillets into the multi-level air fryer basket and place the basket into the instant pot. Seal pot with the air fryer lid. Select air fry mode and cook at 360 F for 10 minutes. Serve.

14-Quick & Easy Salmon

Cook time: 10 minutes | Serves: 2 | Per Serving: Calories 256, Carbs 0g, Fat 13g, Protein 34g

Ingredients:

- Salmon fillets – 2, skinless and boneless
- Olive oil – 1 tsp.
- Pepper & salt, to taste

Directions:

Brush salmon fillets with oil and season with pepper and salt. Place salmon fillets into the multi-level air fryer basket and place the basket into the instant pot. Seal pot with the air fryer lid. Select air fry mode and cook at 360 F for 10 minutes. Serve.

15-Healthy Tuna Patties

Cook time: 10 minutes |Serves: 2 | Per Serving: Calories 416, Carbs 5g, Fat 20g, Protein 48g

Ingredients:

- Cans of tuna – 2
- Lemon juice – 1/2
- Onion powder – 1/2 tsp.
- Garlic powder – 1 tsp.
- Mayonnaise – 1 1/2 tbsps.
- Almond flour – 1 1/2 tbsps.
- Pepper – 1/4 tsp.
- Dried dill – 1/2 tsp.
- Salt – 1/4 tsp.

Directions:

Add all ingredients in a mixing bowl and mix until thoroughly combined. Make four patties from the mixture and place into the multi-level air fryer basket and place the basket into the instant pot. Seal pot with the air fryer lid. Select air fry mode and cook at 400 F for 10 minutes. Serve.

16-Delicious Scallops

Cook time: 7 minutes |Serves: 4 | Per Serving: Calories 170, Carbs 3g, Fat 8g, Protein 19g

Ingredients:

- Scallops – 1 pound
- Basil pesto – 1/4 cup
- Olive oil – 1 tbsp.
- Garlic – 2 tsps., minced
- Heavy cream – 3 tbsps.
- Pepper & salt, to taste

Directions:

Season scallops with pepper and salt and add into the multi-level air fryer basket and place the basket into the instant pot. Seal pot with the air fryer lid. Select air fry mode and cook at 320 F for 6 minutes. Turn scallops halfway through. Meanwhile, in a small saucepan, heat oil over medium heat. Add garlic and sauté for 30 seconds. Add heavy cream and pesto and cook for 2 minutes. Remove saucepan from heat. Add scallops into the large bowl. Pour pesto sauce over scallops and toss well. Serve.

17-Old Bay Seasoned Tilapia

Cook time: 7 minutes |Serves: 2 | Per Serving: Calories 102, Carbs 0.2g, Fat 2g, Protein 21g

Ingredients:

- Tilapia fillets – 2
- Old bay seasoning – 1/2 tsp.
- Lemon pepper – 1/4 tsp.
- Butter – 1/2 tbsp., melted

- Salt

Directions:

Brush fish fillets with butter and season with old bay seasoning, lemon pepper, and salt. Place fish fillets into the multi-level air fryer basket and place the basket into the instant pot. Seal pot with the air fryer lid. Select air fry mode and cook at 400 F for 7 minutes. Serve.

18-Spiced Prawns

Cook time: 6 minutes | Serves: 2 | Per Serving: Calories 81, Carbs 1g, Fat 1g, Protein 15g

Ingredients:

- Prawns – 6
- Chili flakes – 1 tsp.
- Chili powder – 1/2 tsp.
- Black pepper – 1/4 tsp.
- Salt – 1/4 tsp.

Directions:

In a bowl, place prawns, chili powder, pepper, chili flakes, and salt into the bowl and toss well. Add prawns into the multi-level air fryer basket and place the basket into the instant pot. Seal pot with the air fryer lid. Select air fry mode and cook at 350 F for 6 minutes. Serve.

19-Cayenne Pepper Shrimp

Cook time: 6 minutes | Serves: 2 | Per Serving: Calories 196, Carbs 2g, Fat 9g, Protein 25g

Ingredients:

- Shrimp – 1/2 pound, peeled and deveined
- Olive oil – 1 tbsp.
- Paprika – 1/4 tsp.
- Old bay seasoning – 1/2 tsp.
- Cayenne pepper – 1/4 tsp.
- Salt – 1/8 tsp.

Directions:

Add all ingredients into the mixing bowl and toss well. Add shrimp into the multi-level air fryer basket and place the basket into the instant pot. Seal pot with the air fryer lid. Select air fry mode and cook at 390 F for 6 minutes. Serve.

20-Catfish Fish Fillets

Cook time: 20 minutes | Serves: 3 | Per Serving: Calories 286, Carbs 6g, Fat 16g, Protein 24g

Ingredients:

- Catfish fillets – 3
- Fresh parsley – 1 tbsp., chopped
- Olive oil – 1 tbsp.
- Fish seasoning – 1/4 cup

Directions:

Season fish fillets with seasoning and place into a multi-level air fryer basket and place the basket into the instant pot. Seal pot with the air fryer lid. Select air fry mode and cook at 400 F for 20 minutes. Turn fish fillets halfway through. Garnish with parsley. Serve.

21-Coconut Shrimp

Cook time: 5 minutes |Serves: 2 | Per Serving: Calories 272, Carbs 6g, Fat 12g, Protein 32g

Ingredients:

- Shrimp – 8 oz, peeled
- Cayenne pepper – 1/8 tsp.
- Shredded coconut – 1/4 cup
- Almond flour – 1/4 cup
- Egg whites – 2
- Salt – 1/4 tsp.

Directions:

Whisk egg whites in a shallow bowl. In a separate shallow dish, mix together the shredded coconut, almond flour, and cayenne pepper. Dip shrimp into the egg mixture then coat with coconut mixture and place it into the multi-level air fryer basket and place the basket into the instant pot. Seal pot with the air fryer lid. Select air fry mode and cook at 400 F for 5 minutes. Serve.

22-Parmesan Shrimp

Cook time: 10 minutes |Serves: 3 | Per Serving: Calories 251, Carbs 4g, Fat 8g, Protein 37g

Ingredients:

- Shrimp –, 1 pound, peeled and deveined
- Oregano – 1/4 tsp.
- Pepper – 1/2 tsp.
- Parmesan cheese – 1/4 cup, grated
- Garlic cloves – 3, minced
- Olive oil – 1 tbsp.
- Onion powder – 1/2 tsp.
- Basil – 1/2 tsp.

Directions:

Add all ingredients into the large bowl and toss well. Add shrimp into the multi-level air fryer basket and place the basket into the instant pot. Seal pot with the air fryer lid. Select air fry mode and cook at 350 F for 10 minutes. Serve.

23-Simple Tuna Patties

Cook time: 6 minutes |Serves: 4 | Per Serving: Calories 113, Carbs 5g, Fat 2g, Protein 15g

Ingredients:

- Egg – 1, lightly beaten

- Breadcrumbs – 1/4 cup
- Mustard – 1 tbsp.
- Can tuna – 7 oz, drained
- Pepper & salt, to taste

Directions:

Add all ingredients into the mixing bowl and mix until thoroughly combined. Make four patties from the mixture and place into the multi-level air fryer basket and place the basket into the instant pot. Seal pot with the air fryer lid. Select air fry mode and cook at 400 F for 6 minutes. Turn patties halfway through. Serve.

24-Salmon Dill Patties

Cook time: 10 minutes | Serves: 4 | Per Serving: Calories 220, Carbs 10g, Fat 8g, Protein 24g

Ingredients:

- Can salmon – 15 oz, drained and remove bones
- Dill – 1 tsp., chopped
- Breadcrumbs – 1/2 cup
- Onion – 1/4 cup, chopped
- Egg – 1, lightly beaten
- Pepper & salt, to taste

Directions:

Add all ingredients into the mixing bowl and mix until thoroughly combined. Make four patties from the mixture and place into the multi-level air fryer basket and place the basket into the instant pot. Seal pot with the air fryer lid. Select air fry mode and cook at 370 F for 10 minutes. Turn patties halfway through. Serve.

25-Flavorful Tilapia

Cook time: 8 minutes | Serves: 4 | Per Serving: Calories 67, Carbs 4g, Fat 1g, Protein 11g

Ingredients:

- Tilapia fillets – 2
- Dried oregano – 1 tsp.
- Brown sugar – 2 tsps.
- Paprika – 2 tbsps.
- Cayenne – 1/4 tsp.
- Cumin – 1/2 tsp.
- Garlic powder – 1 tsp.
- Salt

Directions:

In a small bowl, mix together cayenne, cumin, garlic powder, oregano, sugar, paprika, and salt and rub all over tilapia fillets. Place tilapia fillets into the multi-level air fryer basket and place the basket into the instant pot. Seal pot with the air fryer lid. Select air fry mode and cook at 400 F for 8 minutes. Turn fish fillets halfway through. Serve.

DESSERTS RECIPES

1-Walnut Brownies

Cook time: 35 minutes | Serves: 6 | Per Serving: Calories 340, Carbs 30g, Fat 23g, Protein 5g

Ingredients:

- Eggs – 2
- Brown sugar – 1 cup
- Vanilla – 1/2 tsp.
- Cocoa powder – 1/4 cup
- Walnuts – 1/2 cup, chopped
- All-purpose flour – 1/4 cup
- Butter – 1/2 cup, melted
- Pinch of salt

Directions:

Spray a baking dish with cooking spray and set aside. In a bowl, whisk together eggs, butter, cocoa powder, and vanilla. Add walnuts, flour, sugar, and salt and stir well. Pour batter into the baking dish. Place steam rack into the instant pot. Place baking dish on top of the steam rack. Seal pot with the air fryer lid. Select bake mode and cook at 320 F for 35 minutes. Serve.

2-Almond Butter Brownies

Cook time: 15 minutes | Serves: 4 | Per Serving: Calories 170, Carbs 22g, Fat 8g, Protein 2g

Ingredients:

- Almond butter – 1/2 cup
- Vanilla – 1/2 tsp.
- Almond milk – 1 tbsp.
- Coconut sugar – 2 tbsps.
- Applesauce – 2 tbsps.
- Honey – 2 tbsps.
- Baking powder – 1/4 tsp.
- Baking soda – 1/2 tsp.
- Cocoa powder – 2 tbsps.
- Almond flour – 3 tbsps.
- Coconut oil – 1 tbsp.
- Sea salt – 1/4 tsp.

Directions:

Spray baking pan with cooking spray and set aside. In a small bowl, mix together almond flour, baking soda, baking powder, and cocoa powder and set aside. Add coconut oil and almond butter into the microwave-safe bowl and microwave until melted. Stir. Add honey, milk, coconut sugar, vanilla, and applesauce into the melted coconut oil mixture and stir well. Add flour mixture and stir to combine. Pour batter into the baking pan. Place steam rack into the instant pot. Place baking pan on top of the steam rack. Seal pot with the air fryer lid. Select bake mode and cook at 350 F for 15 minutes. Serve.

3-Brownie Muffins

Cook time: 15 minutes |Serves: 6 | Per Serving: Calories 70, Carbs 6g, Fat 2g, Protein 8g

Ingredients:

- Cocoa powder – 1/4 cup
- Almond butter – 1/2 cup
- Pumpkin puree – 1 cup
- Liquid stevia – 8 drops
- Protein powder – 2 scoops

Directions:

Add all ingredients into the mixing bowl and beat until smooth. Pour batter into the 6 silicone muffin moulds. Place the dehydrating tray into the multi-level air fryer basket and place the basket into the instant pot. Place muffin moulds on a dehydrating tray. Seal pot with the air fryer lid. Select bake mode and cook at 350 F for 15 minutes. Serve.

4-Delicious Lemon Muffins

Cook time: 15 minutes |Serves: 6 | Per Serving: Calories 202, Carbs 34g, Fat 6g, Protein 4g

Ingredients:

- Egg – 1
- Baking powder – 3/4 tsp.
- Lemon zest – 1 tsp., grated
- Sugar – 1/2 cup
- Vanilla – 1/2 tsp.
- Milk – 1/2 cup
- Canola oil – 2 tbsps.
- Baking soda – 1/4 tsp.
- Flour – 1 cup
- Salt – 1/2 tsp.

Directions:

In a mixing bowl, beat egg, vanilla, milk, oil, and sugar until creamy. Add remaining ingredients and stir to combine. Pour batter into the 6 silicone muffin moulds. Place the dehydrating tray into the multi-level air fryer basket and place the basket into the instant pot. Place muffin moulds on a dehydrating tray. Seal pot with the air fryer lid. Select bake mode and cook at 350 F for 15 minutes. Serve.

5-Vanilla Strawberry Soufflé

Cook time: 15 minutes |Serves: 4 | Per Serving: Calories 50, Carbs 8g, Fat 0.5g, Protein 3g

Ingredients:

- Egg whites – 3

- Strawberries – 1 1/2 cups.
- Vanilla – 1/2 tsp.
- Sugar – 1 tbsp.

Directions:

Spray 4 ramekins with cooking spray and set aside. Add strawberries, sugar, and vanilla into the blender and blend until smooth. Add egg whites into the bowl and beat until medium peaks form. Add strawberry mixture and fold well. Pour egg mixture into the ramekins. Place the dehydrating tray into the multi-level air fryer basket and place the basket into the instant pot. Place ramekins on the dehydrating tray. Seal pot with the air fryer lid. Select bake mode and cook at 350 F for 15 minutes. Serve.

6-Healthy Carrot Muffins

Cook time: 20 minutes │Serves: 6 │ Per Serving: Calories 165, Carbs 33g, Fat 2g, Protein 3g

Ingredients:

- Egg – 1
- Vanilla – 1 tsp.
- Brown sugar – 1/4 cup
- Granulated sugar – 1/4 cup
- Canola oil – 1/2 tbsp.
- Applesauce – 1/4 cup
- All-purpose flour – 1 cup
- Baking powder – 1 1/2 tsps.
- Nutmeg – 1/4 tsp.
- Cinnamon – 1 tsp.
- Grated carrots – 3/4 cup
- Salt – 1/4 tsp.

Directions:

Add all ingredients into a large bowl and mix until thoroughly combined. Pour batter into 6 silicone muffin moulds. Place the dehydrating tray into the multi-level air fryer basket and place the basket into the instant pot. Place muffin molds on the dehydrating tray. Seal pot with the air fryer lid. Select bake mode and cook at 350 F for 20 minutes. Serve.

7-Cinnamon Carrot Cake

Cook time: 25 minutes │Serves: 4 │ Per Serving: Calories 340, Carbs 39g, Fat 19g, Protein 5g

Ingredients:

- Egg – 1
- Vanilla – 1/2 tsp.
- Cinnamon – 1/2 tsp.
- Sugar – 1/2 cup
- Canola oil – 1/4 cup

- Walnuts – 1/4, chopped
- Baking powder – 1/2 tsp.
- Flour – 1/2 cup
- Grated carrot – 1/4 cup

Directions:

Spray a baking dish with cooking spray and set aside. In a mixing bowl, beat sugar and oil for 1-2 minutes. Add vanilla, cinnamon, and egg and beat for 30 seconds. Add remaining ingredients and stir to combine. Pour batter into the prepared baking dish. Place steam rack into the instant pot. Place baking dish on top of the steam rack. Seal pot with the air fryer lid. Select bake mode and cook at 350 F for 25 minutes. Serve.

8-Blueberry Muffins

Cook time: 20 minutes │Serves: 9 │ Per Serving: Calories 343, Carbs 50g, Fat 13g, Protein 5.9g

Ingredients:

- Eggs – 2
- Blueberries – 1 1/2 cups
- Yogurt – 1 cup
- Sugar – 1 cup
- Baking powder – 1 tbsp.
- Flour – 2 cups
- Fresh lemon juice – 2 tsps.
- Lemon zest – 2 tbsps., grated
- Vanilla – 1 tsp.
- Oil – 1/2 cup
- Salt – 1/2 tsp.

Directions:

In a small bowl, mix flour, salt, and baking powder. Set aside. In a large bowl, whisk together eggs, lemon juice, lemon zest, vanilla, oil, yogurt, and sugar. Add flour mixture and blueberries into the egg mixture and fold well. Pour batter into 9 silicone muffin molds. Place the dehydrating tray into the multi-level air fryer basket and place the basket into the instant pot. Place 6 muffin molds on the dehydrating tray. Seal pot with the air fryer lid. Select bake mode and cook at 375 F for 20 minutes. Cook remaining muffins. Serve.

9-Almond Raspberry Muffins

Cook time: 35 minutes │Serves: 6 │ Per Serving: Calories 227, Carbs 13g, Fat 17g, Protein 7g

Ingredients:

- Eggs – 2
- Baking powder – 1 tsp.
- Almond meal – 5 oz
- Coconut oil – 2 tbsps.

- Honey – 2 tbsps.
- Raspberries – 3 oz

Directions:

In a bowl, mix together almond meal and baking powder. Add honey, eggs, and oil and stir until thoroughly combined. Add raspberries and fold well. Pour batter into the 6-silicone muffin molds. Place the dehydrating tray into the multi-level air fryer basket and place the basket into the instant pot. Place 6 muffin molds on the dehydrating tray. Seal pot with the air fryer lid. Select bake mode and cook at 350 F for 35 minutes. Serve.

10-Chocolate Cupcakes

Cook time: 25 minutes | Serves: 9 | Per Serving: Calories 436, Carbs 59g, Fat 19g, Protein 7g

Ingredients:

- Egg – 1
- Cocoa powder – 1/2 cup
- Chocolate chips – 1 cup
- Granulated sugar – 1 cup
- All-purpose flour – 2 cups
- Canola oil – 1/2 cup
- Vanilla – 1 tsp.
- Milk – 1/2 cup
- Yogurt – 1 cup
- Baking soda – 1 tsp.

Directions:

In a mixing bowl, mix together flour, baking soda, cocoa powder, chocolate chips, and sugar. In a large bowl, beat egg with oil, vanilla, milk, and yogurt until smooth. Add flour mixture into the egg mixture and stir to combine. Pour batter into the 9-silicone cake molds. Place the dehydrating tray into the multi-level air fryer basket and place the basket into the instant pot. Place 6 cake molds on a dehydrating tray. Seal pot with the air fryer lid. Select bake mode and cook at 380 F for 25 minutes. Cook remaining cupcakes. Serve.

11-Moist Chocolate Cake

Cook time: 30 minutes | Serves: 4 | Per Serving: Calories 385, Carbs 41g, Fat 24g, Protein 5g

Ingredients:

- Egg – 1
- Canola oil – 1/3 cup
- Baking soda – 1/2 tsp.
- Cocoa powder – 5 tbsps.
- All-purpose flour – 1/2 cup
- Warm coffee – 1 tbsp.
- Vanilla – 1/2 tsp.

- Sour cream – 1/3 cup
- Granulated sugar – 1/2 cup

Directions:

Spray a baking dish with cooking spray and set aside. In a mixing bowl, mix together flour, baking soda, and cocoa powder and set aside. In a small bowl, whisk together egg, vanilla, coffee, sour cream, sugar, and oil. Pour egg mixture into the flour mixture and mix until well combined. Pour batter into the baking dish. Place steam rack into the instant pot. Place baking dish on top of the steam rack. Seal pot with the air fryer lid. Select bake mode and cook at 350 F for 30 minutes.

12-Chocolate Cookie

Cook time: 25 minutes |Serves: 2 | Per Serving: Calories 423, Carbs 44g, Fat 24g, Protein 7g

Ingredients:

- Egg yolk – 1
- Vanilla – 1/4 tsp.
- Granulated sugar – 1 tbsp.
- Brown sugar – 2 tbsps.
- Walnuts – 2 tbsps., chopped
- Chocolate chips – 1/4 cup
- Baking soda – 1/8 tsp.
- All-purpose flour – 1/3 cup
- Butter – 2 tbsps., softened
- Salt – 1/8 tsp.

Directions:

Spray two ramekins with cooking spray and set aside. In a mixing bowl, mix together butter, brown sugar, and granulated sugar. Add vanilla and egg yolk and mix until combined. Add flour, salt, and baking soda and stir to combine. Add walnuts and chocolate chips and stir well. Pour cookie dough into the ramekins. Place the dehydrating tray into the multi-level air fryer basket and place the basket into the instant pot. Place ramekins on a dehydrating tray. Seal pot with the air fryer lid. Select bake mode and cook at 350 F for 25 minutes. Serve.

13-Almond Cranberry Muffins

Cook time: 30 minutes |Serves: 6 | Per Serving: Calories 218, Carbs 17g, Fat 16g, Protein 8g

Ingredients:

- Eggs – 2
- Swerve – 1/4 cup
- Almond Flour – 1 1/2 cups
- Vanilla – 1 tsp.
- Cranberries – 1/2 cup
- Cinnamon – 1/4 tsp.
- Baking powder – 1 tsp.

- Sour cream – 1/4 cup
- Pinch of salt

Directions:

In a bowl, beat sour cream, vanilla, and eggs. Add remaining ingredients except for cranberries and beat until smooth. Add cranberries and fold well. Pour batter into the 6-silicone muffin molds. Place the dehydrating tray into the multi-level air fryer basket and place the basket into the instant pot. Place 6 muffin molds on the dehydrating tray. Seal pot with the air fryer lid. Select bake mode and cook at 325 F for 25-30 minutes. Serve.

14-Chocolate Coffee Cake

Cook time: 15 minutes │Serves: 2 │ Per Serving: Calories 388, Carbs 37g, Fat 25g, Protein 4g

Ingredients:

- Egg – 1
- Black coffee – 1 tbsp.
- Instant coffee – 1/2 tsp.
- Butter – 1/4 cup.
- Cocoa powder – 2 tsp.
- Flour – 1/4 cup
- Sugar – 1/4 cup

Directions:

Spray a baking dish with cooking spray and set aside. In a bowl, beat egg, butter, and sugar. Add black coffee, instant coffee, and cocoa powder and beat well. Add flour and stir to combine. Pour batter into the baking dish. Place steam rack into the instant pot then place baking dish on top of the rack. Seal pot with the air fryer lid. Select bake mode and cook at 330 F for 15 minutes. Serve.

15-Walnut Muffins

Cook time: 15 minutes │Serves: 2 │ Per Serving: Calories 525, Carbs 65g, Fat 26g, Protein 7g

Ingredients:

- Egg yolk – 1
- Walnuts – 2 tbsps., chopped
- Vanilla – 1/8 tsp.
- Sour cream – 1 tbsp.
- Butter – 2 tbsps., melted
- Maple syrup – 3 tbsps.
- Milk – 3 tbsps.
- Ground cinnamon – 1/8 tsp.
- Baking powder – 1/2 tsp.
- Brown sugar – 2 tbsps.
- All-purpose flour – 1/2 cup
- Salt – 1/8 tsp.

Directions:
Spray 2 ramekins with cooking spray and set aside. In a medium bowl, mix together flour, cinnamon, baking powder, brown sugar, and salt. In a separate bowl, whisk together the egg yolk, vanilla, sour cream, butter, maple syrup, and milk. Pour egg mixture into the flour mixture and stir until thoroughly combined. Add walnuts and fold well. Pour batter into the ramekins. Place the dehydrating tray into the multi-level air fryer basket and place the basket into the instant pot. Place ramekins on dehydrating tray. Seal pot with the air fryer lid. Select bake mode and cook at 380 F for 15 minutes. Serve.

16-Easy Chocó Soufflé

Cook time: 15 minutes | Serves: 2 | Per Serving: Calories 601, Carbs 50g, Fat 40g, Protein 10g

Ingredients:
- Egg whites – 2
- Egg yolks – 2
- Sugar – 3 tbsps.
- Flour – 2 tbsps.
- Butter – 4 tbsps., melted
- Vanilla – 1/2 tsp.
- Chocolate – 3 oz, melted

Directions:
Spray 2 ramekins with cooking spray and set aside. In a bowl, beat egg yolks, sugar, and vanilla. Add flour, melted chocolate, and butter and stir well. In a separate bowl, beat egg whites until stiff peak forms. Fold egg white into the egg yolk mixture. Pour batter into the ramekins. Place the dehydrating tray into the multi-level air fryer basket and place the basket into the instant pot. Place ramekins on a dehydrating tray. Seal pot with the air fryer lid. Select bake mode and cook at 330 F for 15 minutes. Serve.

17-Mini Chocolate Cakes

Cook time: 10 minutes | Serves: 4 | Per Serving: Calories 387, Carbs 26g, Fat 29g, Protein 5g

Ingredients:
- Eggs – 2
- Sugar – 3 tbsps.
- Butter –3 oz, melted
- Dark chocolate – 3 oz, melted
- Self-raising flour – 1 1/2 tbsps.

Directions:
Spray 4 ramekins with cooking spray and set aside. In a bowl, beat eggs and sugar until frothy. Add flour, melted chocolate, and butter and fold well. Pour batter into the ramekins. Place the dehydrating tray into the multi-level air fryer basket and

place the basket into the instant pot. Place ramekins on a dehydrating tray. Seal pot with the air fryer lid. Select air fry mode and cook at 375 F for 10 minutes. Serve.

18-Simple & Moist Brownies

Cook time: 20 minutes | Serves: 8 | Per Serving: Calories 294, Carbs 32g, Fat 16g, Protein 4g

Ingredients:

- Eggs – 2
- Nutella – 1 1/4 cups
- All-purpose flour – 1/2 cup
- Salt – 1/4 tsp.

Directions:

Spray a baking dish with cooking spray and set aside. In a bowl, beat together eggs, Nutella, flour, and salt until well combined. Pour batter into the baking dish. Place steam rack into the instant pot. Place baking dish on top of the steam rack. Seal pot with the air fryer lid. Select bake mode and cook at 350 F for 20 minutes. Serve.

19-Perfect Chocolate Brownies

Cook time: 25 minutes | Serves: 8 | Per Serving: Calories 312, Carbs 39g, Fat 17g, Protein 3g

Ingredients:

- Eggs – 2
- Baking powder – 1/4 tsp.
- Cocoa powder – 1/3 cup
- Flour – 1/2 cup
- Sugar – 1 cup
- Olive oil – 1/2 cup
- Vanilla – 1 tsp.
- Chocolate chips – 1/2 cup
- Salt – 1/2 tsp.

Directions:

Spray a baking dish with cooking spray and set aside. In a bowl, mix together flour, baking powder, cocoa powder, sugar, and salt. Add eggs, oil, and vanilla and stir to combine. Add chocolate chips and fold well. Pour batter into the baking dish. Place the steam rack into the instant pot. Place baking dish on top of the steam rack. Seal pot with the air fryer lid. Select bake mode and cook at 350 F for 25 minutes. Serve.

20-Cinnamon Banana Muffins

Cook time: 20 minutes | Serves: 12 | Per Serving: Calories 157, Carbs 22g, Fat 6g, Protein 2g

Ingredients:

- Egg – 1
- Brown sugar – 1/2 cups
- Cinnamon – 1/2 tsp.
- Baking soda – 1 tsp.

- Baking powder – 1 tsp.
- Vanilla – 1/2 tsp.
- Vegetable oil – 1/3 cup
- Mashed banana – 1 1/2 cups
- All-purpose flour – 1 1/2 cups
- Salt – 1/2 tsp.

Directions:

In a large bowl, beat egg, vanilla, oil, and mashed bananas until combined thoroughly. In a separate bowl, mix together flour, baking powder, baking soda, cinnamon, brown sugar, and salt. Pour egg mixture into the flour mixture and stir until combined. Pour batter into the 12-silicone muffin molds. Place the dehydrating tray into the multi-level air fryer basket and place the basket into the instant pot. Place 6 muffin molds on the dehydrating tray. Seal pot with air fryer lid. Select bake mode and cook at 375 F for 20 minutes. Cook remaining muffins. Serve.

21-Moist Strawberry Muffins

Cook time: 14 minutes |Serves: 12 | Per Serving: Calories 167, Carbs 26g, Fat 6g, Protein 2g

Ingredients:

- Egg – 1
- Strawberries – 1 cup, diced
- Sugar – 3/4 cup
- All-purpose flour – 1 1/2 cups
- Milk – 1/2 cup
- Olive oil – 1/3 cup
- Baking powder – 2 tsps.
- Salt – 1/2 tsp.

Directions:

In a large bowl, mix together flour, baking powder, sugar, and salt and set aside. In a small bowl, whisk together egg, oil, milk. Pour egg mixture into the flour mixture and stir to combine. Add strawberries and fold well. Pour batter into the 12-silicone muffin molds. Place the dehydrating tray into the multi-level air fryer basket and place the basket into the instant pot. Place 6 muffin molds on the dehydrating tray. Seal pot with the air fryer lid. Select bake mode and cook at 380 F for 14 minutes. Cook remaining muffins. Serve.

22-Quick Baked Donuts

Cook time: 8 minutes |Serves: 6 | Per Serving: Calories 317, Carbs 59g, Fat 6g, Protein 7g

Ingredients:

- Eggs – 2
- Cinnamon – 1/4 tsp.
- Nutmeg – 1/4 tsp.
- Baking powder – 2 tsps.

- Sugar – 3/4 cup
- Butter – 2 tbsps., melted
- Vanilla – 1 tsp.
- Buttermilk – 3/4 cup
- Flour – 2 cups
- Salt – 1/2 tsp.

Directions:

In a large bowl, beat eggs, butter, vanilla, and buttermilk until combined. In a separate bowl, mix flour, cinnamon, nutmeg, baking powder, sugar, and salt. Pour egg mixture into the flour mixture and stir to combine. Pour batter into 6 silicone donut molds. Place the dehydrating tray in a multi-level air fryer basket. Place the air fryer basket into the instant pot. Place 4 donut molds on the dehydrating tray. Seal pot with the air fryer lid. Select bake mode and cook at 325 F for 8 minutes. Cook remaining donuts. Serve.

23-Nutella Sandwich

Cook time: 5 minutes | Serves: 2 | Per Serving: Calories 341, Carbs 42g, Fat 18g, Protein 4g

Ingredients:

- Bread slices – 4
- Nutella – 1/4 cup
- Butter – 1 tbsp., softened
- Banana – 1, cut into slices

Directions:

Spread butter on one side of each bread slices and place butter side down. Spread Nutella on another side of each bread slices. Place banana slices on 2 bread slices and top with remaining bread slices. Cut the sandwiches in half. Place the dehydrating tray in a multi-level air fryer basket. Place the air fryer basket into the instant pot. Place sandwiches on the dehydrating tray. Seal pot with the air fryer lid. Select air fry mode and cook at 370 F for 5 minutes. Turn sandwiches after 2 minutes. Serve.

24-Chocolate Soufflé

Cook time: 14 minutes | Serves: 2 | Per Serving: Calories 593, Carbs 49g, Fat 40g, Protein 9g

Ingredients:

- Eggs – 2, separated
- Sugar – 3 tbsps.
- Butter – 1/4 cup
- Chocolate – 3 oz, chopped
- All-purpose flour – 2 tbsps.
- Vanilla – 1/2 tsp.

Directions:

Spray 2 ramekins with cooking spray and set aside. Melt butter and chocolate and set aside. In a bowl, beat together sugar, egg yolks, and vanilla. Add melted butter and chocolate. Mix well. Add flour and mix well. In a separate bowl, beat egg whites until soft peaks form. Add 1/3 of egg whites to the chocolate mixture and mix slowly, until all egg whites combine with chocolate mixture. Pour batter into the ramekins. Place the dehydrating tray in a multi-level air fryer basket. Place the air fryer basket into the instant pot. Place ramekins on the dehydrating tray. Seal pot with the air fryer lid. Select air fry mode and cook at 320 F for 14 minutes. Serve.

25-Banana Oat Muffins

Cook time: 10 minutes | Serves: 2 | Per Serving: Calories 192, Carbs 19g, Fat 12g, Protein 2g

Ingredients:

- Banana – 1/4 cup, mashed
- Baking powder – 1/2 tsp.
- Powdered sugar – 1/4 cup
- Butter – 1/4 cup
- Oats – 1/4 cup
- Walnuts – 1 tbsp., chopped
- Flour – 1/4 cup

Directions:

Spray four ramekins with cooking spray and set aside. In a bowl, mix together mashed banana, walnuts, sugar, and butter. In a separate bowl, mix together flour, baking powder, and oats. Add flour mixture to the banana mixture and mix well. Pour batter into the ramekins. Place the dehydrating tray in a multi-level air fryer basket. Place the air fryer basket into the instant pot. Place ramekins on the dehydrating tray. Seal pot with the air fryer lid. Select air fry mode and cook at 320 F for 10 minutes. Serve.

CPSIA information can be obtained
at www.ICGtesting.com
Printed in the USA
BVHW010526101221
623629BV00015B/72

9 781649 842640